PROBLEMS AND PERSPECTIVES IN HISTORY

EDITOR: HUGH F. KEARNEY

Revolution or Evolution
British Government in the Nineteenth Century

Revolution
or
Evolution

British Government
in the Nineteenth Century

Valerie Cromwell

READER IN HISTORY
UNIVERSITY OF SUSSEX

LONGMAN

PROBLEMS AND PERSPECTIVES IN HISTORY

EDITOR: H.F. KEARNEY M.A. PH.D.

A full list of titles in this series
will be found on the back cover of this book

LONGMAN GROUP LIMITED
London

*Associated companies, branches and representatives
throughout the world*

First published 1977

ISBN 0 582 31353 8

Printed in Great Britain
by Whitstable Litho Ltd.

Editor's Foreword

'Study problems in preference to periods' was the excellent advice given by Lord Acton in his inaugural lecture at Cambridge. To accept it is one thing, to put it into practice is another. In fact, in both schools and universities the teaching of history, in depth, is often hindered by certain difficulties of a technical nature, chiefly to do with the availability of sources. In this respect, history tends to be badly off in comparison with literature or the sciences. The historical equivalents of set texts, readings or experiments, in which the student is encouraged to use his own mind, are the so-called 'special periods'. If these are to be fruitful, the student must be encouraged to deal in his own way with the problems raised by historical documents and the historiography of the issues in question and he must be made aware of the wider perspectives of history. Thus, if the enclosure movement of the sixteenth century is studied, the student might examine the historiographical explanations stretching from More's *Utopia* and Cobbett to Beresford's *Lost Villages of England*. At the same time he might also be dealing with selected documents raising important problems. Finally he might be encouraged to realize the problems of peasantries at other periods of time, including Russia and China in the nineteenth and twentieth centuries. In this particular instance, thanks to Tawney and Power, *Tudor Economic Documents*, the history teacher is comparatively well off. For other special periods the situation is much more difficult. If, however, the study of history is to encourage the development of the critical faculties as well as the memory, this approach offers the best hope. The object of this series is to go some way towards meeting these difficulties.

The general plan of each volume in the series will be similar, with a threefold approach from aspects of historiography, documents and editorial consideration of wider issues, though the structure and balance between the three aspects may vary.

A broad view is being taken of the limits of history. Political history will not be excluded, but a good deal of emphasis will be placed on economic, intellectual and social history. The idea has in fact grown out of the experience of a group of historians at the University of Sussex, where the student is encouraged to investigate the frontier areas between his own and related disciplines.

H.F. KEARNEY

Contents

Acknowledgements

We are grateful to the following for permission to reproduce copyright material:

Basil Blackwell Publisher for extracts from *An Introduction to the Principles of Morals and Legislation* edited by W. Harrison; Cambridge University Press and the author L.J. Hume for an extract from his article 'Jeremy Bentham and the Nineteenth Century Revolution in Government' in *Historical Journal Vol.X. No.4. 1967*; Economic History Association for an extract from *Laissez-Faire and State Intervention in Nineteenth-Century Britain* by J. Bartlet Brebner, 1948; Jenifer Hart for extracts from her article 'Nineteenth-Century Social Reform: A Tory Interpretation of History' in *Past and Present Vol.XXXI No.31. 1965*; Her Majesty's Stationery Office for an extract from *British Documents of the Origins of the War 1898-1914, Vol.III* edited by Gooch and Temperley; The London School of Economics and Political Science for an extract from *Our Partnership* by Beatrice Webb; Longman Group Limited for extracts from 'The Waning of the Influence of the Crown' by Archibald S. Foord in *English Historical Review LXII, 1947*; Macmillan Publishers Limited for extracts from *Study of Law of the Constitution* by A.V. Dicey; Oliver MacDonagh for extracts from his article 'The Nineteenth-Century Revolution in Government: A Reappraisal' in *Historical Journal, Vol.1, 1958*; Henry Parris for extracts from his article 'The Nineteenth-Century Revolution in Government: A Reappraisal Reappraised' in *Historical Journal Vol.III, 1960*; Penguin Books Limited for extracts from *The Justice of the Peace* by Esther Moir, (c) Esther Moir, 1969; Alan Ryan for extracts from 'Utilitarianism and Bureaucracy: Views of John Stuart Mill' in *Studies in the Growth of Nineteenth-Century Government* (ed.) G. Sutherland.

Part One
THE PROBLEM

For the most curious fact about this nineteenth-century state is that it never existed. Historians may chase it and try to set limits of time and place upon it, but they do not succeed. It eludes them between the oligarchic maladministration and interfering paternalism of the eighteenth century, on the one hand, and the social service democracy of the twentieth century on the other. For the former was not dead before the latter had been born. If 1870 be taken as a central date public health had already, under the inspiration of Chadwick, begun long since to be accepted as a state charge. So had the control of working conditions. A start was just being made with the creation of a national system of education. And all this was true at a time when the first consistent attempt was being made to put an end to the eighteenth century corruption and privilege, confusion and inefficiency in civil service and administrative organisation.

H.R.G. Greaves, *The Civil Service in the Changing State* (Harrap, 1947), p.9.

This forecast of the difficulties which face any historian who wishes to understand or explain the working of the nineteenth-century British state has proved only too just. The last twenty-five years have seen the publication of many books and articles which have in various ways touched on the changing character of British government in the face of rapidly accelerating industrialization. As more and more work has been done on the mass of material available, the processes of interpretation and analysis of the results of that work have become ever more difficult. The desire to present an easily understood pattern of administrative growth is discouraged by the great variety and complexity of response to the questions historians have asked of their material. The variations between different government departments, the diverse roles of individual officials, the multifarious pressures involved in decision-making, not to mention the unique character of actions taken in specific cases, are all factors which unite to confuse the eager historian.

The problem which has attracted so much attention can be stated quite simply. In 1800 England had virtually no government: the peace was kept and her shores were defended.

3

By 1900 no citizen could fail to be aware of the activities of government. And it was not to be long before signs appeared of a general concern about the dangers inherent in the new situation. As early as 1916 Professor T.F. Tout, the distinguished historian of English administration in the medieval period, was to comment on contemporary trends:

> To us the civil servant is with us always. He rules us from a score of palaces of bureaucracy in Westminster and beyond. Each time that our benevolent rulers extend for our benefit the sphere of state intervention, they are compelled to make a new call on the activity of this ever-increasing class. . . . Our real masters are not the voters. Still less are they the vote-hunting politicians who flit from office to office, either singly or in whole packs. Our masters are the demure and obscure gentlemen in neat black coats and tall hats who are seen every morning flocking to the government offices in Western London at hours varying inversely with their dignity.

> *The English Civil Service in the Fourteenth Century*, (Longmans, 1916), p.3.

Lawyers and political commentators had for some time been conscious of the fundamentally changed role of government and had begun to enquire into how it had all happened. For all his distaste for the depressing situation he described, Tout nevertheless accepted the situation:

> However much we may grumble, this growth of bureaucracy is inevitable. It is in fact a result of the increasing complexity of modern civilization, and is emphasized by the constant growth of state intervention. Time was when a serious effort was made by our grandfathers to realize the ideal of *laissez-faire*; but *laissez-faire* was always much more theory than practice, and in neither relation did it ever come near success.

> *Ibid.*, p.4.

Such assertions as these have come under serious and sustained scrutiny as the results of more recent research have been published. From whatever angle the development of the nineteenth-century state has been considered, historians have in general tended to relate their work to an interpretation of the growth of collectivism, the emergence of the welfare state and to the flowering of a new bureaucracy. A preoccupation with these developments was noticeable before the post-1945 generation of historians demonstrated their interest. The great pioneering work of Sydney and Beatrice Webb produced a monumental series of social and governmental studies. The period just after the First World War saw the publication of the first Whitehall Series of histories of individual government departments, a series which created a most useful framework of information.[1] That series has now been superseded by a second which has brought the departmental histories up to the 1950s. Problems associated with the extension of delegated legislation in the 1930s inspired several enquiries into the background to that extension, the results of which were published in a handful of books and articles in the 1930s and '40s. Since 1945, however, the volume of studies of social reforms and reformers, of the resulting administrative growth and of the changing function of government departments has steadily increased. These works have tended to be descriptive in character and often limited in scope: thus they have been described by one critic, Professor Oliver MacDonagh, who was looking at the problem from a wider and more analytical viewpoint, as 'almost without exception, self-enclosed'.('The nineteenth-century revolution in government: a reappraisal', *Historical Journal*, i[1958], 52). In 1955, F.M.G. Willson made the same point:

> No doubt the most obvious way to begin the charting of so great an area is to tackle institutions piece-meal, to fill the learned journals with close studies of every governmental agency, and thus to provide a mass of evidence from which a pattern of narrative and motive will in time emerge. But to accept this method exclusively would postpone for an indefinite time any study of the machinery of administration as a whole and of the general influences at work in shaping it.

(*Public Administration*, xxxiii (1955), 43.)

[1]See Further Reading, p.219

Nevertheless, despite some conceptual limitations, such descriptive accounts were urgently necessary if any attempts at general conclusions were to be made.

Great pioneering work has been done. Professor Finer's account of the work of Edwin Chadwick, Royston Lambert's study of Sir John Simon, Maurice Wright's and Henry Roseveare's frontier achievements in the Treasury wastes are just a few examples of what has been possible.[2] The wealth of published material now available reveals that in general historians have tended to ask rather the same questions. This is true whether they were writing on the passing of a specific piece of legislation, on the setting up of a new government department, or on the life of an individual who is thought to have been a dynamic influence on policy making. These questions can be pinpointed and defined. What were the pressures behind the given change or innovation? From where did the opposition to administrative growth or innovation come? Why was a particular administrative technique chosen to solve a problem? How efficient was that technique? What was the effect of the various changes?

As different historians have tried to answer these questions about the growth of government in nineteenth-century England, it has become plain that the writing of administrative history must involve a consideration of a vast range of social pressures. The political climate, social and economic developments and current intellectual attitudes are always relevant to the history of administrative change in any society, especially when an attempt is being made to explain the acceptance by that society of an expanding bureaucratic structure. I hope that this will become abundantly clear in this survey of the issues involved in the transformation of nineteenth-century government in England.

[2]See Further Reading, p.218

Part Two

SELECT DOCUMENTS AND COMMENTARIES

I

The Role of Benthamite Ideas in the Growth of Nineteenth-century Government

Recent arguments about the place of Benthamism in the extension of government activities in the first sixty years of the nineteenth century have focused on two separate issues. The first concerns the nature of Jeremy Bentham's views as to the obligations of government to society, particularly in so far as these views were interpreted by A.V. Dicey writing in the early years of the twentieth century. Severe criticisms of Dicey's assumptions about the writings of Bentham were first made by J.B. Brebner in 1948 who argued that Elie Halévy's book, *The Growth of Philosophical Radicalism*, had already proved Dicey wrong. Brebner, who asserted that Dicey had created a myth that Bentham had been the champion of *laissez-faire*, even went so far as to remark that 'Bentham was the archetype of British collectivism' and that in many ways the *Constitutional Code* was the blueprint for a collectivist state.[1] He revealed Bentham as having slowly developed a more empirical approach to the problems of government, coming more and more to accept legislation and control where those powers were necessary to foster human happiness while wishing to protect freedom in

[1] *Journal of Economic History*, supp. viii (1948), 61-2.

any situation where it might ensure such happiness. In 1960, in an article dealing with the influence of Benthamite ideas on nineteenth-century administrative change, Henry Parris criticized Dicey's conclusion that 'though *laissez-faire* is not an essential part of utilitarianism it was practically the most vital part of Bentham's legislative doctrine, and in England gave to the movement for the reform of the law, both its power and its character'.[2] Parris then showed how this misconception encouraged Dicey to look for such influence in the period 1830-70. He concluded that Dicey's 'erroneous beliefs, very closely interwoven with profound perceptions and great wisdom in *Law and Opinion*, have helped to perpetuate a myth about nineteenth-century government — the myth that between 1830 and 1870 or thereabouts, central control in Great Britain was stationary, if not actually diminishing'. In a later article Jenifer Hart supported this view, using in defence of it Bentham's own clear statement that 'in itself Government is one vast evil . . . whenever, by evil thus produced, greater evil is excluded, the balance takes the nature, shape and name of good; and government is justified in the production of it'.[3]

1 Bentham's View of Government

In the here proposed code, of every proposed arrangement, from first to last, without any one exception, the end in view is the greatest happiness of the greatest number. Of the several arrangements in the English system, in no one instance has the greatest happiness of the greatest number been the end in view. At all times, — on every occasion, — in every instance, the end actually pursued by the several sets of rulers, has been the promotion of the particular, and thence sinister, interest of these same rulers. Look the world over, in no one place, — at no one time, has any arrangement of government had for its

[2]H. Parris, 'The Nineteenth-Century Revolution in Government; A Reappraisal Reappraised', *Historical Journal*, iii, (1960), 20,26.
[3]J. Hart, 'Nineteenth-Century Social Reform: A Tory Interpretation of History', *Past and Present*, xxxi, (1965), 48.

object, any other object than the interest of those by whom it has been made. In this case as in every other, in so far as the felicity of the greatest number has been the result, the cause of its being so, is, that in the particular case in question, whilst seeking the insurance of their own personal felicity, it was not in their power to avoid seeking the insurance of the felicity of the greatest number. . .

At no time have the constituent members of the governing body, at no time has the monarch, at no time have the hereditary aristocracy, at no time have the proprietors of seats in the House of Commons, at no time have the clergy, at no time have the judges, had any better endeavour or desire than to swell each of them his own power to its utmost possible pitch. To the weakness of the law taken in its totality, — to its weakness and not to its strength, are the people indebted for everything in their condition, by which they are distinguished from that country in Europe, whatever it be, in which the people are in the most miserable degree oppressed. . .

For, taken by itself, government is in itself one vast evil: only except, in so far as evil, already produced by it, is done away or lessened, can any exercise of government be performed — can the power of government be in any way exercised, but evil is produced by it. But wherever, by evil thus produced, greater evil is excluded, the balance takes the nature, shape and name of good; and government is justified in the production of it.

Financial Law

The financial department, is that by which is performed the extraction, custody, and expenditure of such money and money's worth, as is employed, or professed to be employed, in the public service: viz. in this and the several other branches of the public service.

Whatsoever be the public function, by the exercise of which service is rendered, or pretended to be rendered to the public, or to any part of it; money, or money's worth, or both, are, in a quantity more or less considerable, necessary to be employed and disbursed on the occasion of its being rendered: the financial branch is thus a branch which intertwines itself, and runs through the several other branches of the public service.

11

This branch of government has for its proper end, that branch of good economy which consists of appropriate frugality.

For judging of the consistency of any mass of expenditure with the proper ends of economy, take for a test this directive rule: with the alleged benefit, alleged to be expected from the expenditure, compare the unquestionable burthen produced by a tax to the same amount: forego the benefit, the burthen is excluded. . .

In every department of the public service, good management has two perfectly distinguishable branches: the first peculiar to itself, being correspondent to the particular nature of the service: the other common to it, with all the others, — this universally applying branch of good management is frugality. . .

In a representative democracy, all the several departments having for their actual end good management as applied to each, the financial department has for its actual end frugality, as above defined. . .

Pay of useless offices, pay of needless, overpay of useful offices, pay of sinecures, i.e. of places to which no duty is attached — these are the shapes in which, at the expense of the greatest happiness of the greatest number, money in excess is extracted from the people, for the benefit of public functionaries.

Constitutional Code in *The Works of Jeremy Bentham*, ed. J. Bowring (Edinburgh, 1838-43), Book I, pp.2, 24, 27-32.

Now private ethics has happiness for its end: and legislation can have no other. Private ethics concerns every member, that is, the happiness and the actions of every member, of any community that can be proposed; and legislation can concern no more. Thus far, then, private ethics and the art of legislation go hand in hand. The end they have, or ought to have, in view, is of the same nature. The persons whose happiness they ought to have in view, as also the persons whose conduct they ought to be occupied in directing, are precisely the same. The very acts they ought to be conversant about, are even in a *great measure* the same. Where then lies the difference? In that the acts which they ought to be conversant about, though in a great measure, are not *perfectly and throughout* the same. There is no case in which a private man ought not to direct his own conduct to the production of his own happiness, and of that of his fellow-creatures: but there are cases in which the legislator ought not (in a direct way at least, and by means of punishment applied immediately to particular *individual* acts) to attempt to direct the conduct of the several other members of the community. Every act which promises to be beneficial upon the whole to the community (himself included) each individual ought to perform of himself: but it is not every such act that the legislator ought to compel him to perform. Every act which promises to be pernicious upon the whole to the community (himself included) each individual ought to abstain from of himself: but it is not every such act that the legislator ought to compel him to abstain from.

Where then is the line to be drawn? — We shall not have far to seek for it. The business is to give an idea of the cases in which ethics ought, and in which legislation ought not (in a direct manner at least) to interfere. . .

For the sake of obtaining the clearer idea of the limits between the art of legislation and private ethics, it may now be time to call to mind the distinctions above established with regard to ethics in general. The degree in which private ethics stands in need of the assistance of legislation, is different in the three branches of duty above distinguished. Of the rules of moral duty, those which seem to stand least in need of the assistance of legislation are the rules of *prudence*. It can only be through some defect on the part of the understanding, if a man be ever deficient in point of duty to himself. If he does wrong, there is nothing else that it can be owing to but either some *inadvertence* or some *mis-supposal* with regard to the circumstances on which his happiness depends. It is a standing topic of complaint, that a man knows too little of himself. Be it so: but is it so certain that the legislator must know more? It is plain, that of individuals the legislator can know nothing: concerning those points of conduct which depend upon the particular circumstances of each individual, it is plain, therefore, that he can determine nothing to advantage. It is only with respect to those broad lines of conduct in which all persons, or very large and permanent descriptions of persons, may be in a way to engage, that he can have any pretence for interfering; and even here the propriety of his interference will, in most instances, lie very open to dispute. At any rate, he must never expect to produce a perfect compliance by the mere force of the sanction of which he is himself the author. All he can hope to do, is to increase the efficacy of private ethics, by giving strength and direction to the influence of the moral sanction. . . Without legislation there would be no such thing as a *state*: no particular persons invested with powers to be exercised for the benefit of the rest . . . Private ethics teaches how each man may dispose himself to pursue the course most conducive to his own happiness, by means of such motives as offer of themselves: the art of legislation (which may be considered as one branch of the science of jurisprudence) teaches how a multitude of men, composing a community, may be disposed to pursue that course which upon the whole is the most conducive to the happiness of the whole community, by means of motives to be applied by the legislator.

An Introduction to the Principles of Morals and Legislation, ed. W. Harrison (Oxford U.P., 1960), pp. 414-15, 419-20, 422-3.

2 Dicey's Interpretation of Benthamism

ALBERT VENN DICEY

Throughout his lectures, Dicey asserted the link between Benthamism and individualism or laissez-faire.

These principles, it should be remembered, are not so much the dogmas to be found in Bentham's Works as ideas due in the main to Bentham, which were ultimately, though often in a very modified form, accepted by the reformers or legislators who practically applied utilitarian conceptions to the amendment of the law of England.

It is further clear that the statutes to which reference has here been made, and others like them, have all tended to strengthen that faith in *laissez-faire* which is of the very essence of legislative Benthamism.

Utilitarian individualism, which for many years under the name of liberalism, determined the trend of English legislation, was nothing but Benthamism modified by the experience, the prudence, or the timidity of practical politicians.

But the American Declaration of Independence did, neverthe-less, though in a form open to every logical objection, embody that faith in *laissez-faire* which was in practice the most potent and vital principle of Benthamite reform . . .

This dogma of *laissez-faire* is not from a logical point of view an essential article of the utilitarian creed. A benevolent despot of high intelligence, while admitting that the proper end of scientific legislation is to promote the greatest happiness of the greatest number, might contend that the mass of his people, owing to ignorance and prejudice, did not understand their own interests, and might go on to maintain and act on the principle, that as his subjects were neither the best judges of the conditions which constituted happiness, nor understood the means by which these conditions were to be attained, it was his duty to enforce upon them laws which, though they might diminish individual liberty, were likely nevertheless to ensure the well-being of his people . . . But, though *laissez-faire* is not an essential part of utilitarianism it was practically the most vital part of Bentham's legislative doctrine, and in England gave to the movement for the reform of the law, both its power and its character. At the time when Bentham became the preacher of legislative utilitarianism the English people were proud of their freedom, and it was the fashion to assert, that under the English constitution no restraint was placed on individual liberty which was not requisite for the maintenance of public order. Bentham saw through this cant, and perceived the undeniable truth, that, under a system of ancient customs modified by hap-hazard legislation, unnumbered restraints were placed on the action of individuals, and restraints which were in no sense necessary for the safety and good order of the community at large, and he inferred at once that these restraints were evils.

Lectures on the Relation between Law and Public Opinion in England during the Nineteenth Century (London, 1905), pp. 133, n. 1; 43; 124; 144-6.

3 Dicey's Interpretation Challenged

(a) HENRY PARRIS

Dicey's summary of Benthamism

It must be emphasized in the first place that Dicey does not offer a summary of Bentham's ideas. 'My objects . . . are', he says, ' . . . to sketch in the merest outline the ideas of Benthamism or individualism, *in so far as when applied by practical statesmen they have affected the growth of English law*'. And in a footnote, he goes on to explain that the principles he is about to outline 'are not so much the dogmas to be found in Bentham's works as ideas due in the main to Bentham, which were ultimately, though often in a very modified form, accepted by the reformers or legislators who practically applied utilitarian conceptions to the amendment of the law of England'.

What Dicey himself understood by Benthamism in this special sense is summed up in three words from the passage quoted above: 'Benthamism or individualism'. Variations on this theme recur throughout the book, as these examples show: 'that faith in *laissez-faire* which is of the very essence of legislative Benthamism'. '[Benthamites] looked with disfavour on State intervention . . . Legislative utilitarianism is nothing else than systematized individualism.'

It is obvious that this is a mere travesty of Benthamism. If proof is required, it is supplied by a close examination of Dicey's own argument.

It is a curious question [he says], how far Bentham's own beliefs were directly or logically opposed to the doctrines of sane collectivism. He placed absolute faith in his celebrated 'Principle of Utility'. He held that, at any rate in his time, this principle dictated the adoption of a policy, both at home and abroad, of *laissez-faire*. But it is not clear that Bentham might not in different circumstances have recommended or acquiesced in legislation which an ardent preacher of *laissez-faire* would condemn. It may be suggested that John Mill's leaning towards Socialistic ideals, traceable in some expressions used by him in his later life, was justified to himself by the perception that such ideals were not necessarily inconsistent with the Benthamite creed.

He is aware that Herbert Spencer's argument, that 'the *laissez-faire* doctrine or something very like it, and not the dogma of the "greatest happiness for the greatest number", is the fundamental doctrine of sound legislation', is directed against Bentham.

But the most astounding proof of Dicey's ambivalent attitude towards Bentham's thought is contained in his ninth lecture, which he calls 'The Debt of Collectivism to Benthamism'. He points out that Bentham himself admitted that the principle of utility was dangerous to an unjust society, and 'as in any State the poor and the needy always constitute the majority of the nation, the favourite dogma of Benthamism pointed to the conclusion . . . that the whole aim of legislation should be to promote the happiness, not of the nobility or the gentry, or even of shopkeepers, but of artisans and other wage-earners'. He goes on to note that the consequences of a 'legislative tendency . . . [towards] the constant extension and improvement of the mechanism of government . . . and the increasing application of a new system of centralisation, the invention of Bentham himself, were favoured by Benthamites and promoted utilitarian reforms; but they . . . in fact limited the area of individual freedom'. He points out that 'Benthamites . . . differed among themselves . . . as to the relative important of the principle of utility and the principle of non-interference with each man's freedom. Nominally, indeed, every utilitarian regarded utility as the standard by which to test the character or expediency of any course . . . [and some,] e.g. Chadwick, were practically prepared to curtail individual freedom for the sake of attaining any object of immediate and obvious usefulness, e.g. good sanitary administration'.

The lecture concludes with the following remarkable passage:

The Liberals then of 1830 were themselves zealots for individual freedom, but they entertained beliefs which, though the men who held them knew it not, might well, under altered social conditions, foster the despotic authority of a democratic State . . . Somewhere between 1868 and 1900 three changes took place which brought into prominence the authoritative side of Benthamite liberalism. Faith in *laissez-faire* suffered an eclipse; hence the principle of

17

utility became an argument in favour, not of individual freedom, but of the absolutism of the State. Parliament under the progress of democracy became the representative, not of the middle classes, but of the whole body of householders; parliamentary sovereignty, therefore, came to mean, in the last resort, the unrestricted power of the wage-earners. English administrative mechanism was reformed and strengthened. The machinery was thus provided for the practical extension of the activity of the State . . . Benthamites, it was then seen, had forged the arms most needed by socialists.

Dicey does not argue, then, that *laissez-faire* was the basic principle of Benthamism. Indeed, he admits that 'this dogma of *laissez-faire* is not from a logical point of view an essential article of the utilitarian creed'. What he does argue is that 'though *laissez-faire* is not an essential part of utilitarianism it was practically the most vital part of Bentham's legislative doctrine, and in England gave to the movement for the reform of the law, both its power and its character'. The validity of this thesis can be tested only by an examination of the legislation of the period when, according to Dicey, Benthamism was the dominant opinion.

'The nineteenth-century revolution in government: a reappraisal reappraised', *Historical Journal*, iii, no.1 (1960), 19-20.

(*b*) JENIFER HART

The anti-Benthamites' case rests partly on their views about Benthamism and *laissez-faire*. Many writers have identified Benthamism with 'individualism' and *laissez-faire*; they have observed encroachments on these principles in the sphere of government in nineteenth-century England; and so they have concluded that the Benthamites cannot have been influential. But the Benthamites were not doctrinaire advocates of *laissez-faire*. The main principle of utilitarianism was that the test of policy should be its effect on human happiness. The application of this principle led to considerable extensions of both *laissez-faire* and of state intervention. This has been shown conclusively by Lionel Robbins in a book to which insufficient attention is paid.[1] Thus, writing of Bentham's views on the economic functions of the state, Robbins says that although there is an explicit presumption that, over a wide field, interference is inadvisable, there is no suggestion that it is ruled out *a priori* by some system of natural rights. 'According to the principle of utility . . . the expediency of any act of government must be judged solely by its consequences and not regarded as ruled out in advance by some metaphysical system of rights.' If Bentham's work is considered as a whole, it will be seen that he was 'continually seeking all along the line to erect a structure of institutions, thought out in great detail, within which action is so limited and coordinated as to create the good society'.

It may be asked how such a gross error as identifying Benthamism with *laissez-faire* can have arisen. The answer would seem to be that insufficient attention has been paid to the fact that, while it is true that the Benthamites believed that people always acted in what they conceived to be their interests, of which they were the best judges, they did not think such actions always added up to the greatest happiness of the greatest number: the pursuit of self-interest might not result in social benefits e.g., public health: in such cases it was necessary for the state to intervene. In Roberts' case the error is due partly to incomplete quotation from Bentham . . . Roberts thus ties himself in knots seeing contradictions in Bentham — contradictions between a belief in natural economic laws, and the usefulness of positive legislation and administrative centralization — which in reality do not exist.

'Nineteenth-century social reform: a Tory interpretation of history', *Past and Present*, no. 31 (1965), 47-8.

(c) L.J. HUME

. . . It was a fundamental error to represent Bentham as facing a choice between but two alternatives, 'multiplying, intensifying and fermenting government' and 'its very antithesis'. He himself saw matters in a different light and was free to, and in fact did, select for approval or disapproval different aspects of fermentation or multiplication. And his principles of selection

[1]Lionel Robbins, *The Theory of Economic Policy in English Classical Political Economy* (Macmillan, 1952) see esp. pp. 40-2.

had nothing to do with checks and balances or *laissez-faire* as these are normally understood.

Taken as a whole, the *Constitutional Code* can rightly be interpreted as an attempt to treat law as the fundamental instrument of government, to establish in the legislature a monopoly of legislative activity and authority, to subordinate administrative activity to the legislature, to define and limit the authority and discretion of administrators, and to contribute to the creation of a complete code of law. These objectives sufficiently account for the main features of the system, including those to which Roberts and MacDonagh drew attention. It is unnecessary to introduce *laissez-faire* to explain Bentham's recommendations, and impossible to explain them as part of a system of checks and balances. And his recommendations were not aimed at, nor did they imply, legislative or administrative inactivity or a purely routine kind of administration.

While Bentham sought to limit the powers and the discretion of officials, his model of government and administration was dynamic in a number of respects. At the top, the legislature was given complete discretion and was clearly expected to exercise it freely; the arrangements Bentham proposed for its proceedings are incomprehensible on any other interpretation. Officials were also endowed with certain opportunities and even obligations to exercise initiative. Bentham envisaged them as judging claims and deciding between alternative courses of action with, at crucial points, nothing more than the general utilitarian criterion to guide them. He saw them as encountering new problems and finding new topics for governmental action, as proposing new methods and practices and new legislation, and ultimately perhaps as needing no more than the tacit consent of the legislature to give their proposals the force of law. Dr MacDonagh argued that it was 'a profound change in the presuppositions and bearing of the administrators' when 'in place of a static and purely executive, they developed a dynamic, creative and expert concept of administration'. This is an apt summing-up of the kind of change Bentham was recommending in the *Constitutional Code*.

'Jeremy Bentham and the nineteenth-century revolution in government', *Historical Journal*, x, no. 4 (1967), 375.

4 The Role of Benthamite Ideas: the Nineteenth-century View

A second and much more fundamental disagreement has arisen over what might have been the place of Benthamite ideas in the extension of administrative activity in the nineteenth century. A.V. Dicey and earlier commentators were quite sure that Benthamite influences were of crucial importance in the growth of the nineteenth-century state.

(a) SIR HENRY SUMNER MAINE

Bentham is chiefly concerned with law as it might be and ought to be . . . Bentham aims at the improvement of the law to be effected by the application of the principles now indissolubly associated with his name. Almost all of his more important suggestions have been adopted by the English legislature, but the process of engrafting on the law what to each successive generation seem to be improvements is in itself of indefinite duration, and may go on, and possibly will go on, as long as the human race lasts . . .

No geniuses of an equally high order so completely divorced themselves from history as Hobbes and Bentham, or appear, to me at all events, so completely under the impression that the world had always been more or less as they saw it. Bentham could never get rid of the idea that imperfect or perverse applications of his principles had produced many things with which they had nothing to do . . .

No conception of law and society has ever removed such a mass of undoubted delusion. The force at the disposal of sovereigns did in fact act largely through laws as understood by these Jurists, but it acted confusedly, hesitatingly, with many mistakes and vast omissions. They for the first time saw all that it was capable of effecting, if it was applied boldly and consistently. All that has followed is a testimony to their sagacity. I do not know a single law-reform effected since Bentham's day which cannot be traced to his influence . . .

The capital fact in the mechanism of modern states is the energy of legislatures . . .

To myself the most interesting thing about the theory of

Utility is that it presupposes the theory of Equality. The greatest number is the greatest number of men taken as units; 'one shall only count for one', said Bentham emphatically and over and over again. In fact, the most conclusive objection to the doctrine would consist in denying this equality . . . He saw plainly — nobody more clearly — that men are not as a fact equal; the proposition that men are by nature equal he expressly denounced as an anarchical sophism . . .

I venture to think that this doctrine is nothing more than a working rule of legislation, and that in this form it was originally conceived by Bentham. Assume a numerous and tolerably homogeneous community — assume a Sovereign whose commands take a legislative shape — assume great energy, actual or potential, in this legislature — the only possible, the only conceivable, principle which can guide legislation on a great scale is the greatest happiness of the greatest number. It is in fact a condition of legislation which, like certain characteristics of laws, has grown out of the distance from which sovereign power acts upon subjects in modern political societies, and of the necessity under which it is thereby placed of neglecting differences, even real differences, between the units of which they are composed. Bentham was in truth neither a jurist nor a moralist in the proper sense of the word. He theorises not on law but on legislation; when carefully examined, he may be seen to be a legislator even in morals. No doubt his language seems sometimes to imply that he is explaining moral phenomena; in reality he wishes to alter or re-arrange them according to a working rule gathered from his reflection on legislation. This transfer of his working rule from legislation to morality seems to me the true ground of the criticisms to which Bentham is justly open as an analyst of moral facts.

Lectures on the Early History of Institutions (London, 1875), pp. 343-4, 396-400.

(b) ROLAND K. WILSON

In the preface to his book, 'Law and Public Opinion', A.V. Dicey declared his gratitude to Wilson for conveying to him an impression of the 'immense effect produced by the teaching of Bentham, and also a clear view of the relation between the Blackstonian age of optimism . . . and the Benthamite era of scientific law reform'. Wilson had begun his preface by quoting from Maine: 'I do not know a single Law-Reform effected since Bentham's day which cannot be traced to his influence.'

Influence of Bentham — During all this time Bentham was absolutely unknown to the mass of his countrymen. To the moderately wide class of readers who took an intelligent interest in politics and legislation, he was known as 'a gentleman who wrote bad English and delighted in paradox'. It was only a discerning few who knew him for what he was, studied his works with avidity, and looked up to him as a master, at the same time that they took care not to imitate either the eccentricities of his style or his outspoken, certainly impolitic, and perhaps unjust condemnation of whole classes and professions. Thus, through Parliamentary speeches and a host of pamphlets, reviews and magazine articles, Benthamism began to insinuate itself by driblets into the national mind, while very few knew the source from which it was derived. The presence of this new element is as unmistakable, though of course not so prominent, in the writings of Sydney Smith and Macaulay, of whom the former came very slightly, the latter perhaps not at all, into personal contact with Bentham, as in those of such professed disciples as James Mill and Albany Fonblanque.

The History of Modern English Law (London, 1875), pp. 168-9.

(c) ALBERT VENN DICEY

The acceptance of Benthamism

The existence of a school of thinkers bent on the reform of the law in accordance with utilitarian principles was, as already pointed out, one of the causes which brought the era of quiescence to its close.

Two questions remain for consideration, which to a student of opinion are of profound interest — First, Why did the Benthamite creed obtain ready acceptance? Secondly, What was the extent of that acceptance?

To the inquiry why the teaching of Bentham obtained from,

say 1825 onwards, ready acceptance among thoughtful Englishmen, the right reply, put in the most general terms, is, that when it became obvious to men of common-sense and of public spirit that the law required thorough-going amendment, the reformers of the day felt the need of an ideal and of a programme. Both were provided by Bentham and his school. The ideal was the attainment of the greatest happiness for the greatest number, the programme was to be found in the suggestions for the amendment of the law on utilitarian principles which, during a period of forty years, had been elaborated by Bentham and his disciples. Note, however, that the men who as legislators or writers actually guided the course of legislation were in many instances not avowed Benthamites, and that some of them would have certainly repudiated the name of utilitarians. The law reformers, whether in or out of Parliament — Mackintosh, Brougham, Romilly, Joseph Hume, Grote, Roebuck, Macaulay, O'Connell, Peel, the body of Edinburgh Reviewers, with their ablest representative Sydney Smith — were all at bottom individualists. They were all, consciously or unconsciously, profoundly influenced by utilitarian ideas. But these men were men of the world; they were, even when avowed Benthamites, occupied with and used to the transaction of public affairs; they were most of them members of Parliament; they loved practical compromises as much as Bentham loved logical deductions from strict princi- ples; they were utilitarians, but they accepted not the rigid dogmas of utilitarianism, but that Benthamism of common- sense which, under the name of liberalism, was to be for thirty or forty years a main factor in the development of English law. This liberalism was the utilitarianism not of the study but of the House of Commons or of the Stock Exchange. It modified the doctrines of Bentham, so that, when they were introduced into Acts of Parliament, they were not really carried out to their full extent, and were thus made the more acceptable to the English people. The general answer, then, to the question why Benthamism obtained ready acceptance is that it gave to reformers, and indeed to educated Englishmen, the guidance of which they were in need; it fell in with the spirit of the time.

This answer, however, is very general, not to say indefinite. To state that a creed falls in with the spirit of the time is, after all, nothing but a vague way of asserting that its propagation is aided by favourable conditions. If we are to obtain anything like a definite answer to our inquiry we must examine what were the specific conditions which, say from 1825 onwards, favoured the reception of Benthamite doctrine? They were in part the transitory circumstances of a particular era, and in part certain permanent tendencies of English thought.

Benthamism exactly answered to the immediate want of the day.

In 1825 Englishmen had come to feel that the institutions of the country required thorough-going amendment; but Englishmen of all classes, Whigs and reformers, no less than Tories, distrusted the whole theory of natural rights, and shunned any adoption of Jacobinical principles. The dogmatism and the rhetoric of the French Revolution had even among Radicals lost their charm. The Jacobins or Terrorists, some of whom were still living, had been apostles of the social contract, but the Jacobins were to Englishmen objects of horror — Robespierre was the confutation of Rousseau. The teacher who could lead England in the path of reform must not talk of the social contract, of natural rights, of rights of man, or of liberty, fraternity, and equality. Bentham and his disciples precisely satisfied this requirement; they despised and derided vague generalities, sentiments, and rhetoric; they thoroughly disbelieved in the social contract; nowhere can you find a more trenchant exposure of revolutionary dogmatism than in Bentham's dissection of the 'Declaration of the Rights of Man and the Citizen'.

'The things,' he writes, 'that people stand most in need of being reminded of are, one would think, their duties; for their rights, whatever they may be, they are apt enough to attend to themselves . . . the great enemies of public peace are the selfish and dissocial passions . . . What has been the object, the perpetual and palpable object, of this declaration of pretended rights? To add as much force as possible to those passions, already but too strong, to burst the cords that hold them in; to say to the selfish passions — There, everywhere is your prey! to the angry passions, There, everywhere is your enemy!'

True it is that modern critics might attack Bentham's own teaching as a form of political metaphysics, but his practical

25

ingenuity, his reliance on argument, and his contempt for oratory, concealed from the English world no less than from Bentham himself, the *a priori* and abstract element which lies concealed within Benthamite utilitarianism. Even the prosaic side of Bentham's doctrines, which checks the sympathy of modern readers, reassured sensible Englishmen who in 1830 had come to long for reform but dreaded revolution. Bentham and his friends might be laughed at as pedants, but were clearly not revolutionists; and, after all, whatever were the defects of Bentham as a jurist, critics who really understood his life and work knew that the first of legal philosophers was no agitator, but a systematic thinker of extraordinary power, and a thinker who kept his eyes fixed, not upon vague and indefinite ideals, but upon definite plans for the practical amendment of the law of England. Where could a teacher be found so acceptable to men of commonsense as a lawyer who had studied the law of England more profoundly than had many Lord Chancellors, and had studied it only with a view to removing its defects? He was a teacher of a totally different stamp from a thinker like Godwin, whose revolutionary creed was already out of date; it had been confuted by Malthus, and the theories of Malthus were accepted with fervour by the utilitarians. Bentham was a guide whose speculations lawyers could take seriously, and on whose labours intelligent Englishmen could look with a respect which could not be accorded to the sincere but childish radicalism of Cartwright, to the theatrical bluster of Burdett, to the oratory and egotism of Hunt, or to the inconsistent doctrine and dubious character of Cobbett. Bentham, in short, was a man of wealth and of genius, who had worked out with the greatest logical acumen plans for law reform which corresponded to the best ideas of the English middle class.

About 1830 utilitarianism was, as the expression goes, 'in the air'.

Dr Johnson, the moralist of the preceding generation, had admitted, and Paley, still the accepted English theologian of the day, had advocated, the fundamental dogma of Benthamism, that the aim of existence was the attainment of happiness. The religious teachers who touched the conscience of Englishmen tacitly accepted this doctrine. The true strength of Evangelicalism did not, indeed, lie in the fervour with which its preachers appealed, as they constantly did, to the terrors of hell as a sanction for the practice of virtue on earth, but the appeal was in fact a recognition of the principle of utility. When Bentham applied this principle to the amendment of the law he was in thorough harmony with the sentiment of the time; he gave no alarm to moderate reformers by applying to the appropriate sphere of legislation that greatest happiness principle which the public had long accepted as something like a dictate of common-sense.

The essential strength, however, of utilitarianism lay far less in the transitory circumstances of a particular time than in its correspondence with tendencies of English thought and feeling which have exhibited a character of permanence.

Benthamism fell in with the habitual conservatism of Englishmen.

The Benthamites were, indeed, for the most part democrats, but the most democratic of the utilitarians did not attack any foundation of the English social system. They entertained the prevalent conceptions of individual happiness and of national well-being. To socialism of any kind they were thoroughly opposed; they looked with disfavour on State intervention; they felt no sympathy with those Spencean philanthropists who alarmed the Government in the days of the Six Acts, and the Cato Street Conspiracy; they were more adverse to measures of latent socialism than the Tory philanthropists, represented in literature by Southey, and in the world of practical benevolence by Lord Shaftesbury. The philosophical Radicals proposed to reform the law of England, not by any root and branch revolution, but by securing for all Englishmen the rights of property and of individual liberty which all Englishmen in theory enjoyed, but which, through defects in the law, were in fact denied to large classes. The English public then came to perceive that Benthamism meant nothing more than the attempt to realise by means of effective legislation the political and social ideals set before himself by every intelligent merchant, tradesman, or artisan. The architect who proposes to repair an existing edifice intends to keep it standing; he cannot long be confused with the visionary projector who proposes to pull down an ancient mansion and erect in its stead a new building of unknown design.

Legislative utilitarianism is nothing else than systematised individualism, and individualism has always found its natural home in England.

The strength of Benthamism lay then far less in its originality than in its being the response to the needs of a particular era, and in its harmony with the general tendencies of English thought. This consideration does not detract from the merit of Bentham and his disciples. That in 1830 the demand for reform should arise was a necessity, but a demand does not of itself create the means for its satisfaction. Had not Benthamism provided reformers with an ideal and a programme, it is more than possible that the effort to amend the law of England might, like many other endeavours to promote the progress of mankind, have missed its mark.

What then was the extent to which the Benthamism of common sense or individualism, obtained acceptance?

The answer may be given with certainty and decision. From 1832 onwards the supremacy of individualism among the classes then capable of influencing legislation was for many years incontestable and patent.

This undoubted fact ought not to be concealed from modern students, either by the important consideration . . . that there has always existed a minority who protested against the dogmas of dominant individualism, or by the comparatively unimportant fact that divisions between political parties constantly fail to correspond with real differences of opinion, and that after 1832 Conservatives were often as much imbued with individualism as were Whigs or Liberals. On the passing of the Reform Act, at any rate, the political movement of the day was under the guidance of leaders who, by whatever party name they were known, were in essence individualists and utilitarians. The philosophic Radicals, Grote, Roebuck, and Molesworth, were ardent disciples of Bentham. Brougham, Russell and Macaulay and other Whig statesmen, whether they disclaimed or not the name of Benthamites, were firm believers in common-sense utilitarianism.

Nor is it irrelevant to note that the more closely the renovation of English institutions under the influence of Bentham is studied, the more remarkably does it illustrate the influence of public opinion upon law. Nothing is effected by violence; every change takes place, and every change is delayed or arrested by the influence, as it may seem the irresistible influence, of an unseen power. The efforts of obstructionists or reactionists come to nothing, the toryism of Eldon, the military rigidity of the Duke of Wellington, the intelligent conservatism of Peel, at a later period the far less intelligent conservatism of Lord Palmerston, all appear, though the appearance is in some respects delusive, not in reality to delay for more than periods which are mere moments in the life of nations, the progress of change. On the other hand, the violence of democrats or the fervour of enthusiasts achieves little in hurrying on innovation. In the eighteenth century a duke was ready to recommend universal suffrage. It was demanded by the Chartists, who between 1830 and 1848 seemed destined to carry parliamentary reform to its logical conclusion. Yet now that England is far more democratic than in the middle of the nineteenth century, the electors, who could easily obtain any change which they eagerly desired, acquiesce in arrangements far less democratic than even unqualified household suffrage; and it is arguable (though, be it remembered, many things are arguable which turn out not to be true) that the reforms or changes of the last sixty years have considerably increased the popularity of the Crown, the Peerage, and the Church. If we look then to the changes which have been effected, and what is equally important, to the changes which have not been effected, in the law of the land, we trace everywhere the action of opinion, and feel as if we were in the hands of some mysterious influence which works with the certainty of fate. But this feeling or superstition is checked by the recollection that public opinion is nothing but the opinion of the public — that is, the predominant convictions of an indefinite number of Englishmen.

Law and Public Opinion (London, 1905), pp. 167-74, 175-6, and 208-9.

5 The Challenge to Dicey

The challenge to these views came with the publication in 1958 of an article by Oliver MacDonagh, 'The Nineteenth-century revolution in government: a reappraisal'. In an attempt to unravel what men in the nineteenth century thought and felt contemporary administrative practices should be, MacDonagh passed a number of comments on what he sensed to be incorrect assumptions as to the relationships between Benthamite ideas and the motivations of men involved in the 'nineteenth-century revolution in government'. His own researches on the background to the Passenger Transport Acts had led him to suspect that, when faced with a particular problem, officials tended to adopt an empirical approach to its solution. He asserted that, although Benthamite ideas worked 'altogether with the grain of our "revolution" ', where 'administrative' Benthamism was effective, it 'made a peculiar, idiosyncratic contribution to nineteenth-century administration, and one which was extraneous and at points antagonistic to the main line of growth'. These views encouraged Henry Parris to take up the whole question of the role of ideas in social reform and governmental change. Having surveyed the problems raised by Dicey's misunderstanding of Bentham's ideas, Parris, while agreeing that MacDonagh's model worked in the case of the regulation of emigrant traffic because of a 'peculiar concatenation of circumstances', suggests an alternative model of behaviour: he concludes, 'It would be absurd to argue that Bentham revolutionized the British system of government by power of abstract thought alone. His ideas were influential because they derived from the processes of change going on around him. He was working with the grain. But it does not follow that the same solutions would have been reached had he never lived.' More recent writers on governmental change have tended to accept MacDonagh's arguments, and have been attacked by Jenifer Hart since they 'belittle the rôle of men and ideas, especially the rôle of the Benthamites', and even worse assume 'that opinion in nineteenth-century England was generally humanitarian, and that social evils were attacked and dealt with when people felt them to be intolerable'. She sees the principle of utility as playing a crucial part in the successive battles against vested interests and absurd arguments. More recently, from his work on J.S. Mill, Alan Ryan has further questioned the nature and influence of utilitarianism. And, the debate continues. Why did the men responsible for administrative action and legislative innovation react in the way they did? Were they influenced by received political thought? Was that thought derived from Benthamism?

OLIVER MacDONAGH

An attempt at reconstruction may perhaps best be begun by noting and examining the main elements of explanation. These are, in my view, what men thought, and what men felt, contemporary practices should be (doctrines and sentiments, if one wishes); what external or overt events directed the current of affairs decisively, or made men fully conscious of the tendencies of their time; what the underlying social and economic pressures and the medical, engineering and mechanical potentialities consisted in; and what was actually taking place within executive government itself.

Clearly, these elements belong to different orders of explanation and each has peculiar snares. The first two are explanations in terms of other abstractions, either of an ideological kind such as Benthamism, or of the *Zeitgeist* kind such as humanitarianism. There is an obvious danger of *post hoc propter hoc* in, say, establishing the relationship of the doctrine of utilitarianism to many, if not indeed most 'rational' or 'useful' reforms. And there is an equivalent, if less obvious, danger of forgetting the concealed hen-and-egg problem when a *Zeitgeist* like humanitarianism is said to have produced various pieces of merciful legislation. As Dicey wisely observed, law itself is the creator of law-making opinion. Next, there is the element of explanation which elucidates a concrete event or series of events relevant to governmental change but stops short of considering the operation of the connexions. Thus, a political historian, investigating the waning of the influence of the crown, may discover some pertinent change in the function or distribution of patronage, or in the relationship of the house of commons to executive government, without concerning himself whether public servants were much the same sort of persons, or adopted the same sort of procedures, or did the same sort of things, before and after. This is, of course, no criticism. The political historian is not making it his business to look for or explain possible changes in administration. But, for our present purpose, it is important to draw attention to his omission to do so. Fourthly, there is the element of explanation which looks to the pre-conditions of change, moving back into the vast social and economic hinterland to estimate the problems calling for solution. It may be argued that this is the master factor; that once one has discovered the revolution in the forms of society, one has also discovered the inevitable corresponding revolution in government; that, in the long run, social problems of the nineteenth-century kind will force out the same type of administrative answers, come what may. Up to a point, this is true enough, and much of my later argument is built upon these impulses towards administrative action inherent in particular situations. But it cannot be too strongly emphasized that it is neither a complete answer nor an automatic operation. The correlation between social problem and administrative remedy is seldom exact. The impulse is always prone to be distorted by accidents of personality or ideology or politics, of finance or the state of expert opinion, at the moment when the remedy is debated. Moreover, the mere timing of the particular reforms may have important and even permanent effects upon the whole course of subsequent administration. Just as industries which have developed 'too far too early' find themselves heavily committed to yesterday's processes of production, and vice versa, so there is a very significant element of investment in setting up new government or in consolidating legislation. Finally, there is the silent metamorphosis taking place within such long-established arms of government as the Colonial or Home Offices or the Board of Trade, as new areas of administration were placed under or, we might even say, grew into their jurisdiction. It is enough to remark at this point that a really satisfactory explanation of the governmental revolution must take these unobserved departmental developments into account.

The second fact which emerges from a consideration of these elements of explanation is that our original question, in so far as it has been asked and answered up to the present time, has been asked and answered almost exclusively in terms of the first three. This is so, I think, because Dicey's *Law and Public Opinion*, first in the field, has dominated it ever since. *Law and Public Opinion* is a great book. Other merits apart, it virtually uncovered and stated for the first time the developments which it attempted to explain. But it is the work of a lawyer and a student of political ideas, not that of an historian; and whatever else we find there, we shall not find a *history* of the change in the nature of the state. No public servant is mentioned from beginning to end, unless he were also a political economist or 'thinker'. No reference is made to the cumulative effects of parliamentary investigations or departmental inquiries or reports. The extent to which legislation was actually enforced and the development of the experimental sciences are alike ignored; and a few generalized paragraphs provide the only description of the changes in the size and distribution of the population, and in the domestic and occupational conditions of life. It is political doctrine, trends in articulate opinion, specific statutes marking changes in principle, and the corresponding decisions of the law courts which hold the stage. Dicey does make it clear that the conflict or process was not a conscious one, that despite a plethora of anti-collectivists, there were no pro-collectivists *partout*. None the less, he is absorbed with the abstract and the overt. If he avoids a whig interpretation, if there are no human heroes or villains in his story but simply the unrecognised *Zeitgeist* of collectivism, he none the less (from the historian's standpoint) falls into an equal error, that of intellectualizing the problem altogether.

Many have worked in this field, of course, since Dicey first wrote in 1905. Pre-eminent amongst them is, perhaps, Professor S.E. Finer. Now it is certainly true that his *Chadwick* involves all the elements of explanation which I have outlined. The ideology of utilitarianism; the palpable demonstrations of departures in principle (such as in the Factory Act of 1833); the exact state of things in the new towns and in the relevant experimental sciences; and Chadwick's relations with the politicians, the Poor Law Board's interpretations of the statute, and the conduct of the assistant commissioners in the field, are all interwoven in his narrative. But there are, for our present purposes, two vital omissions. The subject of the inquiry is never administrative change as such, but always a particular person, doctrine, episode or branch of government; and, secondly, however much we may learn about the momentum of administration from his own researches, Professor Finer himself never discusses or draws attention to it. These points apply equally to Mr Lewis's study of Chadwick, and *a fortiori* to the great majority of the other works in this field. By and large, the governmental revolution has not been treated as presenting a distinct and individual problem to nineteenth-century historians, or as involving a distinct and individual process of its own . . . There have been valuable studies of particular departments of state, particular measures, public servants and philanthropists, and some penetrating surveys of the growth of the modern state. But the former are, almost without exception, self-enclosed; and the latter, where they are not merely ideational in bias, interpret growth in an arithmetical and accumulative rather than an organic sense. The truth is that Dicey's is the sole effort to offer on a really considerable scale an explanation of the change as such, and that, although the materials for an answer to the original question have increased prodigiously since 1905, no serious, sustained attempt has been made to formulate an alternative to Dicey's thesis.

In very general terms, the change with which we are concerned is the transformation, scarcely glimpsed till it was well secured, of the operations and functions of the state within society, which destroyed belief in the possibility that society did or should consist, essentially or for the most part, of a mere accumulation of contractual relationships between persons, albeit enforced so far as need be by the sovereign power. Now our first proposition is that very powerful impulses towards such a change were generated by a peculiar concatenation of circumstances in the nineteenth century. Again in very general terms, these circumstances were as follows: the unprecedented scale and intensity and the other novelties of the social problems arising from steam-powered industrialization, and from the vast increase, and the new concentrations and mobility, of population; the simultaneous generation of potential solutions, or partial solutions, to these problems by the developments in mass production and cheap and rapid transport, by the new possibilities of assembling great bodies of labour, skills and capital, and by the progress of the technical and scientific discovery associated with this economic growth; the widespread and ever-growing influence of humanitarian sentiment and of stricter views of sexual morality and 'decency'; the increasing sensitivity of politics to public pressures, and the extraordinary growth in both the volume of legislation and the degree to which its introduction became the responsibility of governments, with the corollaries of changes in parliamentary practice and of the rapid development of parliament's investigatory instruments.

The legislative-cum-administrative process which this con-catenation of circumstances set in motion may perhaps best be described by constructing a 'model' of its operation. Very simply, the most common origin of this sort of process was the exposure of a social evil . . . Once this was done sufficiently, the ensuing demand for remedy at any price set an irresistible engine of change in motion. Once it was publicized sufficiently that, say, women on their hands and knees dragged trucks of coal through subterranean tunnels, or that emigrants had starved to death at sea, or that children had been mutilated by unfenced machinery, these evils became 'intolerable'; and throughout and even before the Victorian years 'intolerability' was the master card . . . Men's instinctive reaction was to legislate the evil out of existence. But at this point the reaction was usually itself resisted. As the threat to legislate took shape, the endangered interests, whatever they might be, brought their political influence into action, and the various forces of inertia, material and immaterial, came into play. Almost invariably, there was compromise. Both in the course of the drafting of the bill, when trade interests often 'made represen-tations' or were consulted, and in the committee stage in parliament, the restrictive clauses of the proposed legislation were relaxed, the penalties for their defiance whittled down and the machinery for their enforcement weakened. None the less the measure, however, emasculated, became law. A precedent was established, a responsibility assumed: the first stage of the process was complete.

The second stage began when it was disclosed, sooner or later, gradually or catastrophically, that the prohibitory legislation had left the original evils largely or perhaps even altogether untouched. For, generally speaking, first statutes tended to be ineffective even beyond the concessions yielded to trade and theory in the course of their drafting and passage. This was so because the draftsmen and the politicians (preliminary parliamentary inquiry in some cases notwith-standing) knew little or nothing of the real conditions which they were attempting to regulate, and paid little or no attention to the actual *enforcement* of penalties and achievements of objects. In consequence, the first act was commonly but an amateur expression of good intentions . . . Simply, the answer was to provide summary processes at law and the like, and special officers to see that they were carried into action; and sooner or later, in one form or other, this was done where mere statute making of the older sort was seen to have been insufficient.

Like the original legislation, the appointment of executive officers was a step of immense, if unforeseen, consequence. Indeed we might almost say that it was this which brought the process into life. There was now for the first time a body of persons, however few, professionally charged with carrying the statute into effect. As a rule, this meant some measure of regulation where before there had been none. It also meant a much fuller and more concrete revelation, through hard experience and manifold failures, of the very grave deficiencies in both the restrictive and executive clauses of the statute; and this quickly led to demands for legislative amendments in a large number of particulars. These demands were made moreover with a new and ultimately irresistible authority. For (once again for the first time) incontrovertible first-hand evidence of the extent and nature of the evils was accumulating in the officers' occasional and regular reports; and there was both a large measure of unanimity in their common-sense recommendations for improvements, and complete unanimity in their insistence upon the urgency of the problems. Finally side by side with the imperative demand for further legislation, there came an equivalent demand for centralization. This, too, arose as a matter of obvious necessity from the practical day-to-day difficulties of their office. For, without a clearly defined superior authority, the executive officers tended towards exorbitance or timid inactivity or an erratic veering between the two . . . Moreover, centralization was quickly seen to be required for two other purposes, the systematic collection and collation of evidence and proposals for reform and the establishment of an intermediary or link between parliament and the executive in the field. Sooner or later, the pressures born of experience succeeded in securing both fresh legislation and a superintending central body. The point at which they did may be taken as the culmination of our third phase.

The fourth stage in the process consisted of a change of attitude on the part of the administrators. Gradually it was borne in upon the executive officers, and through them upon the central authority, that even the new amending, and perhaps consolidating, legislation did not provide a fully satisfactory solution. Doubtless, it embodied many or most of their recommendations and effected substantial improvements in the field concerned. But experience soon showed that it was possible, endlessly possible, to devise means of evading some at least of the new requirements, and equally that the practical effects and judicial interpretations of statutory restrictions could not be always or altogether foreseen . . . All this subtly wrought a *volte face* in the outlook of the administrators. Gradually they ceased to regard their problems as resolvable once for all by some grand piece of legislation or by the multiplication of their own number. Instead, they began to see improvement as a slow, uncertain process of closing loopholes and tightening the screw ring by ring, in the light of continuing experience and experiment. In short, the fourth stage of the process witnessed the substitution of a dynamic for a static concept of administration and the gradual crystallization of an *expertise* or notion of the principles of government of the field in question.

In the fifth and final stage, this new and more or less conscious Fabianism worked itself out into modes of government which seem to us peculiarly modern. The executive officers and their superiors now demanded, and to some extent secured, legislation which awarded them discretions not merely in the application of its clauses but even in imposing penalties and framing regulations . . . In the course of these latest pressures towards autonomy and delegated legislation, towards fluidity and experimentation in regulations, towards a division and a specialization of administrative labour, and towards a dynamic role for government within society, a new sort of state was being born. It was modern in a much fuller and truer sense than even Edwin Chadwick's bureaucracy.

Let us repeat that the development outlined above is but a 'model', and a 'model' moreover which, with a few important exceptions such as slavery reform, applies peculiarly to the half century 1825-75. It does not necessarily correspond in detail with any specific departmental growth. Even in the fields of social reform where it was most likely to operate 'purely', it was not always present. In an exact form, in an unbroken adherence to the pattern, it was perhaps rarely present . . . To sum up, what has been attempted in the preceding section is simply a description, in convenient general terms, of a very powerful impulse or tendency always immanent in the middle quarters of the nineteenth century, and extraordinarily often, though by no means invariably, realized in substance.

To guard further against exorbitance, it may be useful to try to say why this momentum was but relatively effective in its operation. In the first place, the sort of pressures which set the process in motion obviously varied in intensity from field to field . . . True, the process was itself dependent on public and 'parliamentary' opinion in that a certain measure of humanitarianism and of receptivity to the findings of experts and of first-hand experience was a pre-condition of all such change. But, on balance and unless assailed by powerful contrary forces, this opinion tended towards an uncritical acceptance of the *status quo* in law or an uncritical acceptance of the current shibboleths on the corruption, extravagance and inefficiency of government's conduct of any business, and on the proper limits to the state's area of 'interference' . . .

Assuming now the validity of the 'model', subject to these cautions as to its application, what of its usefulness to historians? In general terms, this, it is hoped, is twofold. First, it provides an explanation, or rather a vital part of the explanation, of the catastrophic and very general collapse of political individualism in the last quarter of the nineteenth century. 'We are all socialists now' meant, not of course that the majority or even any significant proportion of the traditionally ruling classes favoured collectivism in any form, but that they were, at last, confronted with the brute *facts* that collectivism was already partially in being and that their society was doomed to move ever further in that direction. To a considerable extent, these brute facts were the product of the governmental momentum which we have described. Although diverted, confined and unrecognized at many points — indeed *because* its nature, extent and tendency towards self-multiplication were unrecognized — the process had spread like a contagion out of sight; and though the collapse of the old idea, or the revelation of its untruth, was naturally a sudden thing, piecemeal contradictions had been accumulating, and the corrosion working steadily for many decades. Dicey's comment on one aspect of this change is profound.

That law creates opinion is plain enough as regards statutes which obviously give effect, even though it may be imperfectly, to some wide principle, but holds at least equally true of laws passed to meet in the readiest and often most offhand manner some pressing want or popular demand. People often, indeed, fancy that such random legislation, because it is called 'practical', is not based on any principle, and therefore does not affect legislative opinion. But this is a delusion.

It is hoped that our 'model' of governmental change has shown that this great truth applies to a very much wider and more complex group of happenings than acts of parliament and the deliverances of courts of appeal.

The second respect in which the 'model' may be useful is in answering the questions posed in the early paragraphs of this essay, namely, the cause and nature of the nineteenth-century change in government. For, in the first place, the very construction of the 'model' indicates that a genuine historical process was involved; and this, it is argued, is a vital change in perspective and a necessary step in understanding the 'revolution'. Secondly, the 'model' provides a centre in relation to which the particular factors can be grouped and the particular developments evaluated. The story becomes at last coherent if we regard it as the norm, and its modification, expulsion or acceleration by exterior forces (however frequent) as a deviation. The relationship of the main factors to the process needs no elaboration now. It will be clear from the course of the preceding argument why, for example, humanitarianism is to be looked on as an indispensable pre-condition of the process, yet in itself both passive and secondary. But the use of the new concept in evaluating particular phenomena and movements in relation to the 'governmental revolution' as a whole may need further explanation; and in an attempt to provide it, we shall try to measure the Northcote-Trevelyan type of reform and Benthamism against our yardstick. For even still it is sometimes assumed that these two between them virtually created the modern form of government.

Now the administrative reform movement of the 1850's derived essentially from that amalgam of Peelism and middle class radicalism which was to form the hard core of the later liberal creed. In the first place, it was a logical follow-through of the Reform Act of 1832; as Gladstone himself put the point, 'This is *my* contribution to parliamentary reform'. For high amongst the objects of many of Trevelyan's supporters were the further loosening of the aristocratic hold on government, and the eradication of those forms of political corruption which had either survived or been generated by 1832. Secondly, it was 'economical reform' as contemporary business men understood the term. A major purpose was the cheapening of government, the simple saving of pounds and pence by the dismissal of superfluous clerks, by getting value for money from the survivors and by those improved 'methods of production' which might be expected to follow from the management of intelligent and conscientious men. Finally, it was impregnated with the radical ethics of self-help and competition. If the fit were to survive, the unfit were to perish: open competition, probation and the single criterion of merit were to establish a species of free trade in public servants. Neither the strange connexions of administrative and educational reform, nor the intertwining of Treasury control and open recruitment, should be allowed to obscure the plain fact that the prime objectives were political and economic . . . it is almost enough to point to the omnipresence of Gladstone, who was in command at the Exchequer or as Prime Minister when each of the major advances along this line of change took place. That is to say, there was a total absence of either bureaucratic or collectivist intention. No increase in public expenditure, no enlargement of the state's field of action, no multiplication of departmental activities was envisaged — quite the contrary. Nor were any alterations in administrative method, other than those implicit in political radicalism and the hoped-for centralization of audit and decision, so much as dreamt of; while the notion that state spending might in any circumstances hasten and not retard the economic growth would have seemed an outrageous foolery. In short, the Northcote-Trevelyan concept of administration was at many points contradictory to ours; and if (and it is still far from proved) open competition and treasury control contributed significantly to the development of the latter, such an outcome was unintentional and would certainly have been anathema to the reformers.

Benthamism is, of course, a very different matter. In its concern with the regulatory aspects of law and the problems of legal enforcement, in its administrative ingenuity and inventiveness, in its downright rejection of prescription, in its professionalism and its faith in 'statistical' inquiry, it worked altogether with the grain of our 'revolution'. Wherever it was the operative force in these respects, it may be said to have displaced or rendered superfluous the administrative momentum. But we must be very circumspect indeed in deciding that Benthamism was the operative force in any particular instance. Broadly speaking, so far as the administrative matters with which we are concerned go, Benthamism had no influence upon opinion at large or, for that matter, upon the overwhelming majority of public servants. It is to a small group of individuals, it is to the actions of a handful of doctrinaires who were placed in positions of high and decisive power, it is to men like Chadwick and Fitzjames Stephen, that we must look almost exclusively for a genuinely Benthamic contribution. In general, nothing is more mistaken than a 'blanket' prima facie assumption that 'useful', 'rational' or centralizing changes in the nineteenth century were Benthamic in origin. On the contrary, the *onus probandi* should rest on Benthamism. The great body of such changes were natural answers to concrete day-to-day problems, pressed eventually to the surface by the sheer exigencies of the case. Indeed, even so apparently idiosyncratic an element as the Panopticon was substantially repeated when, in the late 1840's, the executive officers of both the United Kingdom and New York state emigration commissions (men who had very likely not so much as heard the name of Bentham) independently proposed vast central supervisory offices as the only satisfactory solution to all the difficulties of regulating which bore upon them.

There are moreover other qualifications to be made upon the Benthamic contribution. In the first place, Benthamism in its later form was heavily entangled with two great anti-collectivist influences, political individualism and the notion of the natural harmony of economic interests; and although a few of those who spoke of themselves as utilitarians preserved Benthamism's hard administrative core through thick and thin, this is by no means true of the majority. More important still, even 'administrative' Benthamism had, by the yardstick of our norm, a large measure of eccentricity and irrelevance, mainly through its 'empiricism' and 'science'. As to the first, we can say generally with Professor Oakeshott that 'to understand politics as a purely empirical activity is to misunderstand it, because empiricism by itself is not a concrete manner of activity at all, and can become a concrete manner of activity only when it is joined to something else'. As to the second, even on its own showing Benthamism was scientific only in the sense in which its inquiries were to be conducted in a disinterested and rational manner. What was to be done was classification of data rather than experiment, yet what was to emerge from the inquiry was to be not hypothesis, but dogma. Moreover, the actual investigations made by individual Benthamites were rarely what they pretended to be. They were not exhaustive, but fragmentary; not detached, but heated; not olympian, but doctrinaire. In short, Benthamism was in certain respects none the less *a priori*, generalized and abstract for believing itself to be nothing of the kind. As to the consequences of this illusion for our subject, the abstract atomistic notion of political man led on to the assumptions that a felicific calculus embraced all that the administrator-legislator needed to know, that his law would encounter no unforeseeable or novel obstacle, and that the essence of his work consisted in an initial adjustment of social unbalance and, subsequently, but a maintenance of the equilibrium; while the universalism of the doctrine led on to a fatal disregard of social and political patterns of behaviour, as was apparent, for example, in Chadwick's ill-fated independent Poor Law Board where, in effect, French bureaucracy was torn away from its native context of a division of powers. Thus, generally we can say, first, that the genuine contribution of Benthamism to modern government must be measured in terms of the particular actions of particular individuals; secondly, that Benthamism, in so far as it took colour from other contemporary ideologies, was an obstacle, after their fashion, to the development of modern government; and thirdly, that 'administrative' Benthamism, where it was effective, also made a peculiar, idiosyncratic contribution to nineteenth-century administration, and one which was extraneous and at points antagonistic to the main line of growth.

'The nineteenth-century revolution in government: a reappraisal', *Historical Journal*, i (1958), 54-67.

6 A Defence of the Role of Benthamism: Correctives

(a) J. BARTLET BREBNER

State intervention in nineteenth-century Britain

Even a diagram of the parallels of laissez faire and state intervention during the nineteenth century would be too large to be feasible here, but the principal categories of the latter may be indicated and dated in order to be set against the more familiar examples of the former. Especially noteworthy are the scale and variety of state intervention during the years 1825-1870 which Dicey characterized 'The Period of Individualism'. It is manifestly impracticable to separate the humane, the political, the economic, and the religious objectives of these interventions, or to differentiate sharply one period from another. The one common characteristic is the consistent readiness of interested groups to use the state for collectivist ends.

In the regulation of labor and industry, the century began under the modified Elizabethan statutes and the panicky prohibition of workers' combinations. In 1802 the first Factory Act achieved little to protect 'the health and morals of apprentices' in textile factories, and the repeal in 1813-1814 of important provisions of the Elizabethan statutes as to wages and apprenticeship was followed in 1824-1825 by the legalization of trade-unions and the first ineffectual arbitration act. The Factory Act of 1833 set up Bentham's prescription of central authority and subordinate local inspectors with powers to make and enforce regulations. It was followed next year by a Poor Law (also Benthamite in apparatus) which attempted vainly to prohibit outdoor relief and at the same time to make workhouse life 'less eligible' than any other available employment. The Factory Act of 1833 was followed by a series of similar statutes (chimney sweeps, 1840; mines, 1842; ten hours acts, 1847-1850; etc.) which regulated the workers' hours, safety, education, and so on, thereby building the approaches to state-promoted arbitration of disputes (1867-1896), employers' liability (1880-1897), and minimum wages (1909-1912). The courts repeatedly used interpretations of conspiracy and of the master-servant relationship to wear away statutory legalization of trade-unions, thereby evoking new statutes (Tolpuddle Laborers, 1834; 'New Model' unions, 1851 on; *Hornby* v. *Close*, 1867; Trade Union acts, 1867, 1871, 1875; Taff Vale, 1900; Trade Disputes Act, 1906; Osborne Judgment, 1910; Trade Union Act, 1911; and so on to 1946).

In the promotion and regulation of economic enterprise by the state, there might be listed the railway companies acts from 1823 on, involving compulsory sale of rights of way; abolition of the slave trade (1806) and of slavery (1833); the reformed post office (1840) and nationalization of telegraphs, telephones, and broadcasting (1856-1869, 1878-1911, 1922); inspection and enforcement of standards of amenity, safety, legality, and so forth, in steam power, railways, mercantile marine, gas and water supply, weights and measures, food adulteration, patents, bankruptcy, and so on, by the metamorphosized Board of Trade and the Home Office (after 1825); and the facilitation and regulation of limited-liability joint-stock companies (1856-1862). A great variety of land acts notably restricted freedom of contract in a number of ways.

Closely connected with these activities were the reform and expansion of the civil service which began about 1800 and accelerated greatly with Peel's fiscal reforms (1841-1846) and the revolutions of 1848. There might also be added the so-called 'municipal trading' in markets, docks, water, gas, bathhouses, tramways, electric power, housing, slum clearance, lodging-houses, hospitals, libraries, museums, and so forth, which grew rapidly from about 1850 on. Reform of the criminal law, of other law, of procedure, and of the courts (1816-1873) was regarded by Benthamites as positive state action, and was paralleled by permissive protective police (1829-1839) which became obligatory in 1856.

The 'sanitary idea', or assumption by government (central or local) of preventive responsibility for public health, was originally (1820-1847) promoted by Southwood Smith and Chadwick in pure Benthamite terms and invigorated by the Asiatic cholera which struck England in 1831 and at intervals later, but this centralized program conflicted, not only with endlessly ramified private properties and privileges, but also with jealous local government. Thus their central Board of Health (1848-1854) gave way to local authority, which in turn came under the view of a central Local Government Board in 1871, of a new Sanitary Code in 1875, of a new Local Government Act in 1888, and went back under strong Benthamite central control in the twentieth century.

In some ways the most surprising intervention by the state was in the property and privileges of the Established Church. The exclusive civil and educational privileges of Anglicans were whittled away almost continuously from 1813 to 1891. Parliamentary grants to a Church Building Commission from 1818 on and grants toward education in Ireland furnished the precedents for grants in aid of British education, Anglican and non-Anglican, which expanded enormously from 1833 on to the provision of public education in 1870, which became compulsory in 1880, and free in 1891. The Whig, Sir James Graham, in his popular, but unsuccessful, scheme of 1843 for national education, followed the Benthamite model of the factory and poor law acts, if not the elaboration of Bentham's *Chrestomathia* or the educational provisions of the *Constitutional Code*. Leading Tories and Whigs agreed, but other matters proved more pressing. Marriage was regulated in 1835, divorce in 1857, and burial in 1880. The greatest impact of the state, however, was on church property. The Ecclesiastical Commission of 1836 (further empowered in 1840 and 1850), a kind of perpetual corporation, set out to remedy the scandalous anomalies then existing. Acting on the assumption that the property of the bishops and chapters ought to be employed for the benefit of the church as a whole, they got rid of pluralism, sinecures, and other abuses and reapportioned ecclesiastical income equitably so as to improve the poorer benefices and to establish new ones. A persistent process, also begun in 1836, regulated tithes and church rates.

Other interventions by the state, as, for instance, in provision of small holdings or in extending the legal protection of married women's property from the rich and prudential to the poor and improvident, might be assembled, but the examples above, even if regarded narrowly in their economic aspects, constitute appreciable qualifications of "The Triumph of Laissez Faire." They furnish historical background for A.W. Macmahon's recent assertion that "laissez-faire is quite literally the only untried utopia."

'Laissez faire and state intervention in nineteenth-century Britain', *Journal of Economic History*, supp. viii (1948), 70-3.

(b) HENRY PARRIS

Why should anyone seek to eliminate Benthamism as a factor of importance in nineteenth-century history? A possible answer is that it is one way of resolving an apparent contradiction which has puzzled many students of the subject. Some have discerned contradiction within the theory itself. Halévy, for example, contrasted the principle of artificial identification of interests, on which Bentham founded his theory of politics and law, with the principle of natural identity of interests, which appeared fundamental to his view of economics. Sir Cecil Carr has remarked, 'How the Benthamites could reconcile [their theory of law] with their natural addiction to the doctrines of *laissez faire* is one of the puzzles of political science'. Others have perceived contradictions between theory on the one hand, and the course of events, on the other. Professor Prouty, for example, has written:

> Laissez faire in early nineteenth century Britain was never a system . . . While . . . as a general principle or as an argument against a particular measure [it] might continue to

receive wide publicity, it was persistently defeated in practice . . . The most determined liberal could not consistently argue for laissez faire; he sooner or later found himself advocating a measure which involved the Government in the regulation of some part of industry. State intervention may not have been the policy but it was the growing reality.

Dr MacDonagh is similarly puzzled; he begins one of his valuable papers by saying that it 'is concerned with the extraordinary contrast between this appearance of a "free society" and the realities of the situation'; and ends, 'We have seen how a "despotic" form of administrative discretion came into being almost casually in the very hey-day of liberal individualism and *laissez-faire*'.

An extreme solution to this problem was propounded by the late Professor Brebner. His attitude to Dicey resembles that of Marx towards Hegel. Dissatisfied with his argument, he sought to correct it by turning it the other way up. Dicey had assumed that the consequences of Benthamism were limited, in practice, to the promotion of *laissez-faire*. Brebner suggests, on the other hand, that 'laissez faire was a political and economic myth in the sense formulated by Georges Sorel'. But 'although laissez faire never prevailed in Great Britain or in any other modern state, many men today have been led to believe that it did. In this matter . . . Dicey . . . seems to have been the principal maintainer of the myth for others.' *Law and Opinion* 'amounted to an argument against increasing collectivism. The lectures were so passionately motivated as to be a sincere, despairing, and warped reassertion of the myth in terms of legal and constitutional history . . . In using Bentham as the archetype of British individualism he was conveying the exact opposite of the truth. Jeremy Bentham was the archetype of British collectivism.' Developments of *laissez-faire* did of course take place; but these Brebner attributes to a separate current of opinion, deriving ultimately from Adam Smith, and though often working in alliance with Benthamism, never assimilated to it.

Valuable as a corrective to Dicey, Brebner's argument is too violent a reaction against it. The twin themes of his paper — *laissez-faire* and state intervention — were equally characteristic developments of the middle quarters of the nineteenth century, and it is not necessary to assume that they were in contradiction to one another. Professor Robbins has shown how they were reconciled in the field of economic theory. He denies Halévy's argument that there was a contradiction between the assumptions underlying Bentham's theory of law, on the one hand, and classical economics, on the other. The latter was not based on an assumed identity of interests. 'If [the classical economists] assumed anywhere a harmony, it was never a harmony arising in a vacuum but always very definitely within a framework of law . . . they regarded the appropriate legal framework and the system of economic freedom as two aspects of one and the same social process.' They advocated free enterprise as the general rule in economic affairs on the grounds that it was the system most likely to benefit the consumer. But they recognized no natural right of free enterprise. Like any other claim to freedom, it had to be justified by the principle of utility. As a rule, it was so justified; but there were many situations (e.g. where producers enjoyed a monopoly) where the State should intervene.

Historical Journal iii, (1960), 33-5.

7 Some Comments on MacDonagh's 'Model' and a New Look at Dicey's Interpretation

HENRY PARRIS

His summary of legislation in the middle decades of the nineteenth century

Dicey has no difficulty, of course, in producing a number of examples to show that Benthamism influenced the trend of legislation in the period 1830-70 in the direction of individualism and *laissez-faire*. It is not necessary here to say more about such events as the repeal of the Corn Laws than that their significance is recognized. What is important is to examine Dicey's treatment of those events which do not fit into his general thesis; for example, factory inspection, exchequer grants for education, the New Poor Law, and other similar measures.

Dicey is under no illusions about the importance of factory legislation for the validity of his thesis: it was here, he tells us, that 'Benthamite liberalism suffered its earliest and severest defeat'. He attempts to explain it (or explain it away) by two lines of argument. First, he attributes it to a current of opinion hostile to Benthamism: 'the factory movement gave rise to a parliamentary conflict between individualism and collectivism'. But he does not seriously argue that such men as Oastler, Sadler and Shaftesbury were exponents of a coherent philosophy of society, comparable with Benthamism. Indeed, he has already told us that collectivism 'cannot, in England at any rate, be connected with the name of any one man, or even . . . any one definite school'. Secondly, he attributes it to a force which he labels 'Tory philanthropy'. The Factory Movement 'from the first came under the guidance of Tories. With this movement will be for ever identified the names of Southey, Oastler, Sadler and above all of Lord Shaftesbury.' No one will dispute this statement in its application to the men named as individuals, but the attempt to stick a party label on the movement soon fails. Dicey himself quotes Shaftesbury on the hostility of three leaders of his party — Peel, Graham and Gladstone — to the Ten Hours Bill, while admitting 'Nor was there anything in the early factory movement which was opposed either to Benthamism or to the doctrines of the most rigid political economy'. In illustration of this admission, he points to the support of McCulloch (1833), Cobden (1836) and Macaulay (1846).

In discussing the assumption by the State of a share of the responsibility for elementary education, Dicey adopts a different line of argument. He points out that this departure in policy dates from 1833. He is quite clear, too, about its relevance to his theme: 'our present system [of elementary education] is a monument to the increasing predominance of collectivism'. What, then, were the currents of opinion which led to the foundation of this monument? None worth discussing, it seems; Dicey chooses the first exchequer grant for education as his example of the way in which 'a principle carelessly introduced into an Act of Parliament intended to have a limited effect may gradually so affect legislative opinion that it comes to pervade a whole field of law'. It is true, of course, that the historic vote of

49

17 August 1833 was passed by a very small House; but to suggest that there was anything casual about the interest which such men as Hume and Roebuck were taking in education at the time is to ignore the vital role played by education in the whole system of Benthamite thought. But Dicey was scarcely capable of understanding the part of such a man as Hume; for him, 'no politician was a more typical representative of his time than Joseph Hume. He was a utilitarian of a narrow type; he devoted the whole of his energy to the keeping down or paring down of public expenditure.' Yet Hume criticized the 1833 grant, not because it was too big, but because it was too small . . .

With all his ingenuity, Dicey found himself in some difficulty when he came to fit the New Poor Law into his chosen categories: 'it may appear to be a straining of terms if we bring under the head of freedom in dealing with property the most celebrated piece of legislation which can be attributed to the philosophic Radicals. The Poor Law of 1834 does not, on the face of it, aim at securing freedom of any kind; in popular imagination its chief result was the erection of workhouses, which, as prisons for the poor, were nick-named Bastilles.' He recognizes that the effect of the 1834 Act was to increase the power of the State: 'the new Poor Law . . . placed poor relief under the supervision of the State'. And again 'the rigorous and scientific administration of the Poor Law (1834) under the control of the central government . . . [was a measure which] limited the area of individual freedom'.

Dicey's division of the nineteenth century into three periods in the relation between law and public opinion

It may seem merely pedantic solemnly to consider whether Dicey was right in discerning three periods into which his subject could be divided. What can it matter, one may ask, whether there were three periods or only two — or for that matter, four? The question is of importance, however, because most of the distortions of his argument are closely bound up with his determination to demonstrate distinct trends in opinion and legislation before and after 1870. His three periods are as follows: (i) Legislative Quiescence, 1800-30. (ii) Period of Benthamism or Individualism, 1825-70. (iii) Period of Collectivism 1865-1900.

Dicey himself was in considerable difficulties about his second turning-point. Speaking of the 'characteristics of law-making opinion in England' he lays down a general proposition that 'the opinion which affects the development of the law has, in modern England at least, often originated with some single thinker or group of thinkers. No doubt it is at times allowable to talk of a prevalent belief or opinion as "being in the air", by which expression is meant that a particular way of looking at things has become the common possession of all the world. But though a belief, when it prevails, may at last be adopted by the whole of a generation, it rarely happens that a widespread conviction has grown up spontaneously among the multitude.'

This has an obvious application to the role played by Bentham and his school in the transition from the first to the second period. But when Dicey comes to the next point of transition he cannot point to anyone who played a similar part: 'hence a curious contrast between the mode in which an inquirer must deal with the legislative influence on the one hand of Benthamism, and on the other hand of collectivism. He can explain changes in English law by referring them to definite and known tenets or ideas of Benthamite liberalism; he can, on the other hand, prove the existence of collectivist ideas in the main only by showing the socialistic character or tendencies of certain parliamentary enactments.'

Nor is Dicey any more successful in pointing to the date when the period of individualism gave place to the period of collectivism. Since all division of the past into periods is artificial, it would be reasonable to say that these periods shade so insensibly into one another, that no precise turning-point can be fixed. But Dicey does not do that. 'The difference', he tells us, 'between the legislation characteristic of the era of individualism and the legislation characteristic of the era of collectivism is, we perceive, essential and fundamental. The reason is that this dissimilarity (which every student must recognize, even when he cannot analyse it) rests upon and gives expression to different, if not absolutely inconsistent, ways of regarding the relation between man and the State.' So

51

profound a change should be capable of being precisely dated, and in fact when the period of collectivism is first introduced we learn that it began in 1865.

Unfortunately, at other points in the argument a number of other dates are mentioned. Let us review them in receding order of time. 'Socialistic ideas were, it is submitted, in no way a part of dominant legislative opinion earlier than 1865, and their influence on legislation did not become perceptible till some years later, say till 1868 or 1870, or dominant till say 1880.' 'At this point [i.e. the Limited Liability legislation of 1856-62] individualistic and collectivist currents of opinion blend together . . . [since] the transference of business from individuals to corporate bodies favours the growth of collectivism.' 'In 1854 the opponents of Benthamism were slowly gaining the ear of the public.' Collectivist influence is to be seen in housing legislation, dating from 1851; in municipal trading, from 1850 onwards; and in public health legislation, from 1848 onwards. 'At the time when the repeal of the corn laws gave . . . what seemed to be a crowning victory to individualism . . . the success of the Factory Acts gave authority . . . to beliefs which, if not exactly socialistic, yet certainly tended towards socialism or collectivism.' 'Between 1830 and 1840 the issue between individualists and collectivists was fairly joined. Elementary education 'is a monument to the increasing predominance of collectivism.' It dates from 1833.

Hence, on Dicey's own showing, the era of collectivism began in 1833, only three years after the end of the period of legislative quiescence.

But how, it will be asked, could a man of Dicey's undoubted ability, learning and wisdom be wrong? That he could, on occasion, be wrong, not in small details, but in questions of great moment closely related to his special field of study, we know from his treatment of *droit administratif* in France and the alleged absence of administrative law in England. In *Law and Opinion* he was working in a field not entirely his own: 'An author who tried to explain the relation between law and opinion during the nineteenth century undertook to a certain extent the work of an historian.' And he recognizes that there are limits to the degree to which 'an English lawyer ought . . . to trespass . . . upon the province of historians, moralists, or philosophers'. He was aware, moreover, of the peculiar difficulty attendant on his inquiry: 'few indeed have been the men who have been able to seize with clearness the causes or the tendencies of events passing around them'. Even those who have come nearest to success have usually missed something of first-rate importance; and he instances Bagehot's lack of reference to the importance of political parties . . .

Dicey, then, writing his lectures at the end of the nineteenth century, made no attempt to go beyond the accepted accounts of what took place two generations before, either in regard to what men were thinking or to what men were doing. He believed that, since he was 'writing of a time not long past, [he] was almost delivered from the difficulty with which an historian of eras removed by the lapse of many years from his own time often struggles in vain, the difficulty, namely, of understanding the social and intellectual atmosphere of bygone ages'. But he was born in 1835, and on his own admission, his memory of public affairs went back only to 1848 . . .

Halévy has described the intellectual atmosphere in which the young Dicey grew up:

> Thus was developed in England, twenty years after Bentham's death, a new and simplified form of the Utilitarian philosophy. Disciples of Adam Smith much more than of Bentham, the Utilitarians did not now include in their doctrine the principle of the artificial identification of interests, that is, the governmental or administrative idea; the idea of free-trade and of the spontaneous identification of interests summed up the social conceptions of these new doctrinaires, who were hostile to any kind of regulation and law . . . While Darwin was extending Malthus' law to all living species, Buckle reduced the whole philosophy of history to the principles of Adam Smith's political economy. In his *Social Statics*, Herbert Spencer expressly assimilated the natural laws of the economists with the natural law of the jurists . . . He regarded with the same scorn both the meddling Conservatism of Lord Shaftesbury and the meddling Radicalism of Edwin Chadwick: both demanded the intervention of governmental authority in social relations, and this was enough to make them both stand condemned.

These trends in thought were paralleled in the world of administration. Chadwick finally left the field of Poor Law in 1847. By the Act of 1844, the factory inspectors lost their power to make regulations and act as magistrates, and until 1878, the number of inspectors failed to keep pace with the number of factories liable to inspection. The abandonment of the Railway Regulation Bill in 1847 marked the turning-point in the trend towards greater public regulation of railways, which was not resumed for another two decades. With Kay-Shuttleworth's departure from the Education Department in 1849, his policy of central control of voluntary grant-aided schools was tacitly abandoned; and following the adoption of 'payment by results' in 1862, explicitly reversed.

This, however, was the climate of opinion in which Dicey's ideas were formed. He wrongly supposed that it had existed since about 1830. His erroneous beliefs, very closely interwoven with profound perceptions and great wisdom in *Law and Opinion*, have helped to perpetuate a myth about nineteenth-century government — the myth that between 1830 and 1870 or thereabouts, central control in Great Britain was stationary, if not actually diminishing.

If anything of a structure survives a bombardment, it is likely to be the foundations. So it is in this case. The criticism advanced above has left untouched three of Dicey's most important arguments: that there is a close connexion between law and opinion in general; that that connexion was particularly close in the case of Benthamism; and that the practical influence of Benthamism dates from the period 1825-30. Although Dr MacDonagh does not explicitly criticize Dicey's views on any of these points, his own argument implies a rejection of them . . .

His model allows for public opinion in the ordinary sense of the term; that is, the sort of popular sentiments and attitudes to particular questions of the day that are today assessed by the Gallup poll. But it has no place for opinion, as Dicey understood the term, either in general or in the particular case of Benthamism. 'Broadly speaking, so far as the administrative matters with which we are concerned go, Benthamism had no influence upon opinion at large or, for that matter, upon the overwhelming majority of public servants . . . In general, nothing is more mistaken than a "blanket" prima facie assumption that "useful", "rational" or centralizing changes in the nineteenth century were Benthamic in origin.' . . . If it is wrong to assume that men were influenced by Bentham's ideas, it is equally wrong to assume, as Dr MacDonagh does, that they were not. The one contention like the other, needs to be supported by evidence, and this he does not supply. His omission is scarcely surprising, since it is almost always more difficult to prove, historically, a negative than a positive; it none the less weakens his argument. Moreover, public administration is a field where all men are very definitely not equal. It is quite true that the contribution of the obscure and the anonymous should not be overlooked; but one Chadwick (whose Benthamism Dr MacDonagh admits) counted for more than many hundreds of rank and file public servants.

In any case, Dr MacDonagh makes no allowance for the unconscious influence of ideas on men's minds.

> Indeed, even so apparently idiosyncratic an element as the Panopticon was substantially repeated when, in the late 1840's, the executive officers of both the United Kingdom and New York state emigration commissions (*men who had very likely not so much as heard the name of Bentham*) independently proposed vast central supervisory offices as the only satisfactory solution to all the difficulties of regulating which bore upon them.

It is a mere assumption that these men were not consciously following Bentham's precepts. The resemblance between their proposals and the Panopticon could be used with equal effect to support the hypothesis that they were Benthamites. However, it is far more likely that, without having heard of him, they were unconsciously influenced by Bentham's thought, which had by the period in question become very widely diffused. If Dr MacDonagh seriously contends that a man's ideas can affect the course of events only through those who have heard his name (and presumably have some knowledge of his beliefs), few indeed would be the thinkers who could be shown to have had any practical influence at all. The influence of Freud and Keynes, for example, would be factors barely worth the notice of the contemporary historian . . .

Having applied the MacDonagh model to the creation of the Metropolitan Police in 1829, the appointment of the first factory inspectors in 1833, the setting up of the Poor Law Commissioners in 1834, and concluded that it does not fit the pattern of development, Parris continues;

The administrative changes considered so far all originated before 'the middle quarters of the nineteenth century'. It might be supposed that the model would work more smoothly in the case of those which originated after 1825, so that it would operate solely within the period where it is said peculiarly to apply; but this is not so. A 'peculiar concatenation of circumstances' led to initial legislation during this period in a number of important fields, of which five examples may be cited: regulation of railways (1840), inspection of mines (1842) and steamships (1846), public health (1848), and the administration of exchequer grants to local police forces (1856). In all these cases, the first statutes provided also for the appointment of officers to administer them. The model requires that officers should be appointed because men had learnt from experience. Before 1825, men acquired the experience but did not learn from it; after 1835, they gave themselves no time to learn from experience, but appointed enforcement officers at once. Dr MacDonagh seems to anticipate this criticism when he says that 'the stages into which the process has been divided [are not] to be regarded as sacrosanct . . . or indeed anything more than the most logical and usual type of development'. But this will not do. He also insists, with complete justification though uncharacteristic diffidence, that 'we might almost say that it was [the appointment of executive officers] which brought the process into life'. If, therefore, this 'step of immense . . . consequence' was not taken as the result of experience, some other explanation must be found.

It is not far to seek. After about 1835 a demonstration effect came into existence between different branches of the central administration. The example of the first enforcement officers had set the pattern, and it became normal to appoint them simultaneously with the first incursion into a new field. The Education Committee of the Privy Council, for example, with its inspectors, was organized by Kay-Shuttleworth, who had transferred to the new department in 1839 from service under the Poor Law Commissioners. It was natural that he should be influenced by the methods he had learnt in his old department in setting up the new. Dr MacDonagh's model could easily be adapted to allow for this demonstration effect, if it could be shown that emigration regulation influenced other branches of administration. But, on his own showing, there is no reason whatever to suppose it did. It was 'an obscure . . . branch of the administration . . . which had not even a distinctive name . . . no considerable attention was ever drawn upon its officers. Indeed, by and large, the British public was unaffected by, and probably ignorant of, its existence.' When other services came to be set up, they were modelled on such well-publicized exemplars as the Metropolitan Police, factory inspection, and the New Poor Law, and thus came under the indirect influence of Benthamism.

To sum up: Dr MacDonagh's model fits well enough the facts of emigrant regulation. Indeed, it would be strange if it did not, for that appears to be the sole branch of administration from which it derives. But in considering the development of ten other branches of administration, not one has been found where there is even a reasonable degree of fit between model and reality . . .

Following this lead, it is possible to suggest a model which avoids the difficulties inherent in those discussed above, while taking into account all the facts enumerated. Its stages are as follows:

(a) The nineteenth-century revolution in government, though a response to social and economic change, cannot be understood without allowing for the part played in it by contemporary thought about political and social organization; to adopt Dicey's terminology, there was a close connexion between law and opinion.

(b) In the relationship between law and opinion, the nineteenth century falls into two periods only, with the dividing line about 1830.

(c) Throughout the second of these periods, the dominant current of opinion was Utilitarianism.

(d) The main principle of Utilitarianism was what its

supporters themselves believed and asserted — the principle of utility. The application of this principle led to considerable extensions both of *laissez-faire* and of State intervention simultaneously.

(e) Once special officers had been appointed to administer the law, they themselves played a leading role in legislation, including the development of their own powers.

It is unnecessary to add much in elaboration of what has already been said. The first stage (as also the last) incorporates factors which Dicey ignored, and to which Dr MacDonagh rightly calls attention. But there is nothing inevitable about the process by which institutions respond to changes in the society around them. The nineteenth-century revolution in government was one example of such a response; the French Revolution, and the Hitler regime, were others. One essential factor differentiating the three situations is the nature and quality of current thought about society, its problems, and their solution. It would be absurd to argue that Bentham revolutionized the British system of government by power of abstract thought alone. His ideas were influential because they derived from the processes of change going on around him. He was working with the grain. But it does not follow that the same solutions would have been reached had he never lived.

The second point does not deny that there was a change in the tone of legislation after about 1870. But it resulted from such factors as the Great Depression, the extension of the franchise, and pressure from the administration itself, rather than from the adoption of a hypothetical philosophy of collectivism. Utilitarianism was at work throughout — 'that current of thought which arises in Bentham at the beginning of the century and flows into Fabianism at its end'.

The fourth point may appear something of a paradox. Yet at the time, there were those who believed in both principles simultaneously. Nassau Senior, for example, believed in *laissez-faire*, but not in the 'nightwatchman' conception of the State:

> many political writers . . . have declared that the business of government is simply to afford protection, to repel, or to punish, internal or external violence or fraud, and that to do more is usurpation. This proposition I cannot admit. The

only rational foundation of government . . . is expediency — the general benefit of a community. It is the duty of a government to do whatever is conducive to the welfare of the governed.

So celebrated an advocate of State intervention as Chadwick still allocated a large, though limited, area to private enterprise:

He had great faith in self-interest. He commended it as the spring of individual vigour and efficiency; and it figures prominently in his thought as the most persistent and calculable element in human character. But he saw no evidence at all that social benefits resulted of necessity from its pursuit, and much which persuaded him that without the barriers erected by the law its undirected energies might disrupt society. He put his trust, therefore, not in the rule of some 'invisible hand' blending the interests of the individual and society in a mystic reconciliation, but in the secular authority of the State which, abandoning the superstitions of *laissez-faire*, should intervene to guide the activities of individuals towards the desirable goals of communal welfare.

When, therefore, existing institutions were subjected to the test of utility the result might be either more free enterprise or less. When it was asked 'Do the Corn Laws tend to the greatest happiness of the greatest number?' the answer (in 1846) was 'No'. When it was asked 'Since free competition does not work in the field of railway enterprise, would public regulation tend to the greatest happiness of the greatest number?' the answer (in 1840) was 'Yes'. The question was then, as indeed it is today, not *laissez-faire or* State intervention, but where, in the light of constantly changing circumstances, the line between them should be drawn.

Dr MacDonagh has done well to draw the attention of administrative historians to the importance of factors which Dicey did not take into account. Some of these were external, such as economic and technical change; others were internal, for example, the influence of the administrators on legislation. Few would deny the importance of these factors, although little has been done so far to work out their implications in detail. In this respect, his studies of the regulation of emigrant traffic are important pioneer work. He has shown that it is possible to account for the development of one minor branch of central administration without considering the influence of Benthamism. But he has not shown that other branches developed in a similar way, as would be necessary to sustain his thesis that Benthamism was a factor of, at most, very minor importance. The accepted view holds the field; namely, that the nineteenth-century revolution in government, though not attributable to Benthamism as sole cause, cannot be understood without allotting a major part to the operation of that doctrine.

Historical Journal, iii, (1960), 20-37.

8 The Climate of Opinion

JENIFER HART

The second idea I wish to examine is that opinion in nineteenth-century England was generally humanitarian, and that social evils were attacked and dealt with when people felt them to be intolerable.

MacDonagh in his 'model' article says that 'throughout and even before the Victorian years "intolerability" was the master card. No wall of either doctrine or interest could permanently withstand that single trumpet cry, all the more so as governments grew ever more responsive to public sentiment, and public sentiment ever more humane.' He repeats the same idea in his book. 'It was very likely that legislation to stamp out the "intolerable" miseries and mortalities of the Atlantic passage would sooner or later be enacted: "intolerability" would sooner or later open any door.' . . .

But does this idea get us anywhere? It purports to be an explanation of why certain things happened, but it is not really an explanation at all. It is a tautology. For what else does one mean when one says the public found something 'intolerable' than that they took steps, or supported steps, to change it or to eradicate it? Moreover even if the alleged explanation is not so interpreted as to escape condemnation as a tautology, it is open to at least two other objections. Firstly there was no agreement as to what was intolerable, since there was agreement neither as to the criteria of what was or was not intolerable, nor even as to the bare facts. For example the hours worked in factories seemed in the eighteen thirties intolerable to many workers, whereas to Nassau Senior the long hours were practicable because of the extraordinary lightness of the labour. Edward Baines and others too in the forties insisted that the work was light. Bright and Cobden thought in 1846 that the philanthropists would pamper the people. And as late as the sixties and seventies, after exhaustive, impartial enquiries had taken place into many industries, several M.P.s said that the evils had been much exaggerated. Similarly the miners felt they could only tolerate the physical and mental strain and the extreme unpleasantness of their work if they confined their working week to five or five and a half days; but Tremenheere, the first mines inspector, thought it was wrong for them to take two days off each week, even though they earned less by doing so. Nor was there agreement as to whether work in mines was prejudicial to the health of children; Ashley and other philanthropists of course thought it was, whereas the mine owners considered it was not. Nor did this attitude obtain only in the forties when the subject was new: it was still in evidence in the sixties and seventies. Indeed as late as 1892, the general manager of some collieries, referring to labour in the mines generally, said before the Royal Commission on Labour: 'Coal mining is not an unhealthy occupation. The atmosphere in which the miner works is temperate, and of necessity fresh and comparatively pure. The coal miner is not liable to . . . wet and dry . . . He is liable to accidents of various descriptions', but he added that there was a considerable number of workmen between the ages of fifty-five and seventy still following their occupations. For many people this would not have been the criterion of tolerability. Even on public health — a field in which most people by 1848 were convinced something should be done — there was a good deal of disagreement about the facts: thus it was said that the Health of Towns Association and the various Commissions of Enquiry had exaggerated the evils, though no doubt few went so far as the vestry which in

1849 said cholera was a weak invention of the enemy — cholera which had killed 80-90,000 persons in Great Britain in 1848-9. This kind of thing shows the extreme difficulty in getting agreement on the facts or on the criteria by which one should judge them.

A second objection to the 'intolerability' thesis is that it is so elastic it can never be proved false. Its proponents talk of a 'trumpet cry which could not be permanently withstood' and say it would 'sooner or later open any door'. This is rather like Marx's theory of the inevitability of revolution, or Toynbee's declining civilizations. Neither of them commits himself to a time schedule and thus cannot be proved wrong by the argument that what they have predicted or postulated has not yet happened. Moreover the time necessary for the removal of an 'intolerable' state of affairs might be very great. Even the field studied by MacDonagh supports this: it took fifty years to secure tolerable conditions in emigrant ships. Many people in the early eighteen forties thought it intolerable to employ boys under the age of thirteen underground, but this continued until 1900 when it was forbidden by statute. Similarly many people from the forties onwards thought the accident rate in mines intolerable and reducible, but very little improvement was effected until the last decade of the century.

As to humanitarianism, Kitson Clark considers there was a general tendency towards humanitarianism and reform in most classes in the country throughout the reign of Queen Victoria; he writes of 'the conscience . . . of the nineteenth century' and of a 'strong sense of social responsibility' . . .

These phrases are objectionable because either they are so vague as to be useless, or, if they are taken to mean something, namely that most people or most important people were humanitarian, they are false or at any rate misleading . . .

Take factories for example: no one could deny that there were some philanthropists in this field, but there were also many employers who would not comply with the safety measures prescribed by the law . . . The long battles the inspectors had with employers on this issue can leave no doubt that many employers were extremely callous. It was no answer, in the inspectors' views, to say, as the employers did, that people were careless: death or mutilation were too severe punishments for heedlessness and indiscretion. And anyway it was precisely because people were careless that one should protect them.

Or take mines: the inspectors attributed accidents in the fifties largely to the faults of the proprietors and managers . . . It was no good appealing to the higher feelings of the managers, as they had none. The only possible approach seemed to be through self-interest: to point out that the sacrifice of labour must in the long run increase the average cost . . . in the seventies, one of the inspectors was still very depressed: the safety of the men was little thought of when it stood in the way of a few shillings more profit, e.g. proper pit props were often not provided because of the expense . . .

Nor does the treatment of poverty suggest a great advance in the sentiment and practice of humanity, although many of the people concerned with it conceived they were thinking about the best interests of the recipients . . .

The tendency to think of the nineteenth century as more humanitarian than it was may be partly explained by identifying a concern for morality with a concern for happiness. Thus Tremenheere considered he was a humanitarian, but in fact he was really a moralist. He was not shocked by the hardness and unpleasantness of the labour of miners, or by the accident rate: what shocked him was their drunkenness, sensuality, laziness, extravagance, and lack of respect for their masters . . . Charles Trevelyan . . . thought much more about the demoralizing effects of charity than about the diminution of pain; dependence on others was a moral disease. We can agree that he inherited something from Evangelicanism, but this was its distrust of pleasure and ease, and high valuation of work and effort, rather than its humanitarian strain.

Overstress on humanitarianism can also be explained by misconceptions about the doctrines of the churches and the effect generally of religion in the nineteenth century . . .

(i)   Some causes may appear superficially to have been religiously inspired, but were not;

(ii)   many Christians were not interested in social or political problems at all;

(iii) the influence of religion was often hostile rather than conducive to social progress.

Finally I wish to turn to the wider views thrown out by these Tory historians. For their study of nineteenth-century English history has led them to make certain generalizations about how things happen: viz. that somehow they happen all by themselves, as a result of chance, of 'the historical process', or of 'blind forces', and that they are not planned or even the result of human agency . . .

All these views are misleading and indeed dangerous in their implications. They are misleading because they conceal certain ambiguities. For instance when Kitson Clark talks of 'man' ('possibly no man can control' impersonal historical forces), it is not clear whether he means one man, or men in general. Many things, e.g. social conditions in towns, are admittedly not controllable by one man, or even by a small number of men, but are in principle controllable by men in general, as contrasted with some things that are not so controllable at a given level of technical knowledge, e.g. physical phenomena such as the weather or earthquakes . . . It is true of course that what happens may be affected by the machinery of administration which exists (e.g. a system of inspection and reports), but ultimately that machinery is created by men, and worked by men, and what happens is due to people making decisions, even if only decisions not to alter the machinery.

These views are dangerous when applied to evil happenings because they encourage what Sir Isaiah Berlin calls 'the great alibis'. The social effects of the Industrial Revolution were caused in the final analysis by men, by men's inventiveness, by men's decisions to build factories, by men's desires to make profits . . . Maybe we should not pass moral judgments on them if they did not intend evil; but we should not go on from there to say that the evils were not caused by people. Moreover in some instances the action taken by men so much aggravated the effects of an already existing evil that it comes very near to men intending evil. For instance, take tenement housing: the increase in population in the nineteenth century created possibilities of making money out of housing the working classes which had not existed earlier. A house would be converted into numerous dwellings, and when new buildings were erected the same plan was copied. The people who built tenements were not blind: they did it consciously in order to make money . . . There are of course greater problems of evidence which arise in connection with the past than with the present, but the issue is not in principle different, and historians who suggest that it is confuse issues and are liable to do harm by undermining notions of responsibility.

Moreover these views are dangerous because they lead imperceptibly to the notion that it is better not to plan: because so much was achieved unplanned, the process can and should be repeated. Unplanned changes are spoken of as 'natural', a praise word. Social progress, it is implied, will take place in the future as in the past without human effort as a result of 'the historical process'. The role of men and of ideas (whether for good or for bad) is belittled: we are, as it were, just drifting at the mercy of chance and of blind forces; but all will turn out for the best because of a generally diffused humanitarianism. The only way of testing the validity of this advice is empirically by examining the evidence offered by the past. And in so far as social reform in nineteenth-century England is concerned, the evidence seems to suggest that most social evils were not removed without fierce battles against absurd arguments, vested interests, obscurantism and timidity, and that their removal required considerable effort and determination on the part of men (even if only of obscure men) who realized that it was worth while making a conscious effort to control events. And in this enterprise many of them were assisted, whether they knew it or not, by Benthamism in spite of all its shortcomings, in the sense not so much of practical and ingenious answers to particular problems (though these were important), but in the sense of the humanist notion that the diminution of misery is in itself a sufficient justification for action, and that reforms need not be justified on the ground they improve the morality of the sufferer.

Past and Present, no.31 (1965), 48-54, 57-61.

9 The Ambiguity of the Utilitarian Attitude to Bureaucracy

ALAN RYAN

To descend from the theory to the instance, I must say a few words about the case of nineteenth-century administrative reform in particular. At this level of specificity, the obvious question is: To what extent can we explain the changes in the organization, recruitment and functions of the English bureaucracy as the result of deliberate planning by ideologically sophisticated reformers? One recently popular answer is, to no extent at all. There are two distinct strands in what, following MacDonagh, we may call the 'anti-ideational' case. The first is a plainly empirical argument to the effect that changes in the range of tasks performed by government and in the machinery by which these tasks were performed took place according to no plan whatever. The process was one of incoherently responding to the felt pressure of events — abuses were discovered, were felt to be 'intolerable', were remedied ineffectively, then tackled more effectively; the social and political effects of all this were cumulative, and none too clearly perceived, although they were such as to move English society in the 'collectivist' direction that Dicey described. But this was essentially a process which no-one foresaw and which no-one involved in it would have supported had he understood it to be in train. On this argument I have only two comments. The first is that it *is* essentially a factual matter how the various areas of bureaucratic regulation came to grow and thus that it is a matter which awaits resolution by empirical investigation. The second is that it follows from this that we cannot *a priori* show MacDonagh's account, when it is generalized to provide a 'model', to be any more plausible than what would be my own guess — that different departments probably had very different histories. The tone, rather than the content, of MacDonagh's 1958 article leads me to suspect that he subscribes to some more general philosophy of history which plays down the role of ideas in the causation of events. But in the absence of any explicit and argued statement of this philosophy and the grounds on which it rests, I cannot judge whether it would rule out influences of the kind I hope to elucidate below or not. The second aspect of the anti-ideational case presents no problem, for it is the claim that, no matter what the actual processes, they were not inspired by utilitarian aims and the ideals, and that these latter had no great part in bringing about administrative reform. To regard the series of nineteenth-century reforms as Benthamite is to ignore the facts — they were neither inspired by Bentham and his followers nor did they proceed in accordance with their hopes. On this issue, my conclusions hereafter will be mostly negative. I am inclined to think that there was no such thing as *the* utilitarian view on administrative reform, no such thing as *the* utilitarian view of the proper role of government and the best mode of its fulfilling that role — any more, I suspect, than there was any such thing as *the* non-conformist view or *the* evangelical view. Rather, what was involved in accepting a utilitarian view of social and political life was the acceptance of a theoretical framework within which certain ways of describing and explaining social and political matters got to the heart of them; it did not involve the possession of answers to problems of social and political practice so much as the assurance that certain ways of posing these problems was the right way of posing them. Where there were answers to be had, it involved the belief that certain reasons for thinking them to be answers were, in principle, good reasons. But, it is plain enough that many of the assumptions of utilitarianism were up to a point at home in other ways of perceiving the world· — for example, in unitarianism after Priestley — a fact which must then have rendered communication as much easier as it now renders the ascription of influence more difficult. And, a final *caveat*, at the level of biographical adequacy, we must remember that all of us are subject to the influence of more ways than one of looking at the world, so that among the ideas to be found in the minds of secular utilitarians there will be ideas that come from other, quite foreign sources — foreign, that is, to the calculus of pleasure and pain. In this respect, as in others, John Stuart Mill has an obvious claim on our attention.

For our present purposes, Mill's views have several aspects of some interest. As all the world knows, he was a man whose mind had supposedly been made for him by a utilitarian education amounting to indoctrination, but who spent his life deliberately exposing himself to influences of which his mentors would often have disapproved. Mill's views thus show us how utilitarian doctrines could be strengthened and weakened by influences from such unlikely sources as Coleridge's romantic conservatism, Saint-Simon's managerial positivism, and the continental liberalism of von Humboldt and de Tocqueville. Again, Mill was a man both of the study and the office, and while this is no way lessens the primacy of his intellectual achievements, it does mean that when he talks about government he speaks from thirty years' experience of earning his living as an administrator. In the *System of Logic*, Mill defended his father against the charge of being an impractical doctrinaire by pointing out how extremely practical his father had been when involved in the world of everyday business. And the same claim could be made on behalf of the son. Indeed, anyone who thinks that a concern for the theoretical foundations of politics is necessarily a disqualification for practical life would do well to think hard about the more than adequate services rendered to the East India Company by James and J.S. Mill.

Before we turn to the final flurry of Mill's career, when he defended the Company against the government's plans for its dissolution in 1858, there is one further matter on which the Company's activities shed some light. This is the problem of why utilitarians were so ready to defend its administrative activities, if they were, as Dicey believed, enthusiasts for an individualist and laissez-faire creed. The problem has been more or less effectively dissolved by Dr Parris's re-examination of Dicey's views; but it is worth stressing the difference between a doctrine which is as a matter of logic both atomistic and mechanistic and one which supports either a romantic or a rugged individualism. So far as the *logic* of utilitarianism goes, the only questions we can ask about private versus public initiative are questions of relative cost and efficiency. There is no reason to suppose that the earlier utilitarians recoiled from the public provision of any particular good for any reason other than their belief that it would be wasteful; and certainly there is in Bentham none of that enthusiasm for individual liberty which is so characteristic a feature of the writings of J.S. Mill. Much the strongest objection to public enterprise seems to have stemmed from hostility to the aristocratic incumbents of governmental positions who could be calculated to turn the public service into a series of jobs for their friends. The creation of an honest and patronage-free bureaucracy would in principle have gone a long way towards meeting the objection.

Although I have said, and stand by having said, that there was no such debate in progress as the debate between individualists and collectivists, there is one distinction worth introducing at this point that relates to the substance of that argument. Mill was aware of the danger of a benevolent oppression in democracy in a way which was foreign both to Bentham and James Mill, and almost as foreign to enthusiasts for spiritual community like T.H. Green. Mill was afraid of the stifling of individuality, a deadening of initiative, especially in moral and intellectual matters; and it was this fear of social oppression more than a fear of political oppression that dominated *Liberty*. When discussing the matter in that essay, Mill drew two different lines along which we might oppose governmental interference. One ground for resisting is that the activity in question is simply not the business of society at large — not, at any rate, in the sense that society has any right to coerce people into some particular line of conduct; the other ground is that although the action does fall into the domain of public business, the odds are that government, being clumsy and expensive, will do more harm than good by intervening, at any rate coercively. These are very different kinds of objection, for the former is an absolute moral prohibition on control and coercion, while the latter is technical only. Mill, however, takes great care to leave room for governments to act non-coercively, in collecting and circulating information, offering advice and helping private efforts — in other words, there is no antipathy to collective action as such — except when it is collective coercion. This means that Mill's views to some extent cut across the usual line of debate. For instance, he was emphatic that the state ought to intervene very strenuously in making parents responsible for the health, education and welfare of their children, but adamant that neither government nor society at large was entitled to enquire into the religious beliefs of teachers, members of parliament and so on. A propos of the usual arguments about collectivism, we ought, on this evidence, to be careful to distinguish the libertarian argument about the undesirability of government activity in some areas of a sacrosanct kind from the utilitarian argument about probable ineffectiveness of government activity. Mill, on this reading, was both more and less of a collectivist than his father and Bentham had been — more in wanting government to take a kind of cultural lead that they never expected of it, but less in that he attached as they did not a positive value to doing things for oneself wherever possible. Strictly speaking, there is not much place in utilitarianism for this sort of argument for the intrinsic merits of self-rule. It was a notion imported into utilitarianism from outside — Mill's sources being Coleridge's concern for self-culture and von Humboldt's enthusiasm for untrammelled self-expression.

There is no such thing as *the* utilitarian view of bureaucracy, either in the advocacy of more rather than less government or in pressing the claims of expertise against those of public opinion — and vice versa. It is not even the case that there is a single account to be given of the nature of expertise; utilitarianism is ambiguous between depicting the expert as a man who knows what will maximize the general welfare and who ought therefore to be allowed a free hand to manage our lives and depicting the moral arena as one in which free beings make what claims they can on the right to tell experts (who possess a wholly factual kind of knowledge) what goals to pursue, and what policies to implement — and here of course there is no question of the existence of 'moral expertise'. Behind these ambiguities lie the following considerations: to be a theory of any degree of generality, a moral theory like utilitarianism must be able to capture and explain moral attitudes which were not initially couched in utilitarian terms. So utilitarianism tends — as do religious creeds and any other ethical system — to stretch the notions of pleasure and pain in order to accommodate what began as other values. This, I should emphasize, is not to say that there is nothing distinctive about utilitarian ethics, any more than the observation that Aristotelian and Newtonian physics both explain many of the same phenomena would support the argument that they were indistinguishable. What, indeed, I hope that this essay has shown is how the reformer's problems appear, when they appear in a distinctively utilitarian guise.

'Utilitarianism and bureaucracy: the views of J.S. Mill', in G. Sutherland ed., *Studies in the Growth of Nineteenth-century Government* (Routledge, 1972), pp. 36-7, 38, 46-7, 56-8, 61-2.

II

The Nature of British Government in 1800

The 'economical reformers' of the 1780s had drawn the attention of the House of Commons to the range of pensions and sinecures available to ministers of the Crown for the encouragement of political support. They had also had in mind the unnecessary expense of such offices. But, as Dunning explained to the Commons when supporting the reduction of the Civil List, 'But the saving of money, is but a secondary object. The reduction of the influence of the crown, is the first.' Professor A.S. Foord has demonstrated the way in which royal patronage was eroded in the years before 1830. Henry Parris and Henry Roseveare in their studies of the civil service and the Treasury respectively have provided yet more evidence.

10 The Arguments for Reform in 1780

EDMUND BURKE

Mr SPEAKER — I rise, in acquittal of my engagement to the House, in obedience to the strong and just requisition of my constituents, and, I am persuaded, in conformity to the unanimous wishes of the whole nation, to submit to the wisdom of Parliament 'A Plan of Reform in the Constitution of Several Parts of the Public Economy.' . . .

But what, I confess, was uppermost with me, what I bent the whole force of my mind to, was the reduction of that corrupt influence which is itself the perennial spring of all prodigality and of all disorder — which loads us more than millions of debt — which takes away vigor from our arms, wisdom from our councils, and every shadow of authority and credit from the most venerable parts of our Constitution . . .

Besides this, Sir, the private enemies to be made in all

attempts of this kind are innumerable; and their enmity will be the more bitter, and the more dangerous too, because a sense of dignity will oblige them to conceal the cause of their resentment. Very few men of great families and extensive connections but will feel the smart of a cutting reform, in some close relation, some bosom friend, some pleasant acquaintance, some dear, protected dependant. Emolument is taken from some; patronage from others; objects of pursuit from all . . .

We have, Sir, on our establishment several offices which perform real service: we have also places that provide large rewards for no service at all. We have stations which are made for the public decorum, made for preserving the grace and majesty of a great people: we have likewise expensive formalities which tend rather to the disgrace than the ornament of the state and the court. This, Sir, is the real condition of our establishments . . . I therefore lay down to myself seven fundamental rules: they might, indeed, be reduced to two or three simple maxims; but they would be too general, and their application to the several heads of the business before us would not be so distinct and visible. I conceive, then,

First, That all jurisdictions which furnish more matter or expense, more temptation to oppression, or more means and instruments of corrupt influence, than advantage to justice or political administration, ought to be abolished.

Secondly, That all public estates which are more subservient to the purposes of vexing, overawing, and influencing those who hold under them, and to the expense of perception and management, than of benefit to the revenue, ought, upon every principle both of revenue and of freedom, to be disposed of.

Thirdly, That all offices which bring more charge than proportional advantage to the state, that all offices which may be engrafted on others, uniting and simplifying their duties, ought, in the first case, to be taken away, and, in the second, to be consolidated.

Fourthly, That all such offices ought to be abolished as obstruct the prospect of the general superintendent of finance, which destroy his superintendency, which disable him from foreseeing and providing for charges as they may occur, from preventing expense in its origin, checking it in its progress, or securing its application to its proper purposes. A minister, under whom expenses can be made without his knowledge, can never say what it is that he can spend, or what it is that he can save.

Fifthly, That it is proper to establish an invariable order in all payments, which will prevent partiality, which will give preference to services, not according to the importunity of the demandant, but the rank and order of their utility or their justice.

Sixthly, That it is right to reduce every establishment and every part of an establishment (as nearly as possible) to certainty, the life of all order and good management.

Seventhly, That all subordinate treasuries, as the nurseries of mismanagement, and as naturally drawing to themselves as much money as they can, keeping it as long as they can, and accounting for it as late as they can, ought to be dissolved. They have a tendency to perplex and distract the public accounts, and to excite a suspicion of government even beyond the extent of their abuse.

Under the authority and with the guidance of those principles I proceed — wishing that nothing in any establishment may be changed, where I am not able to make a strong, direct, and solid application of those principles, or of some one of them. An economical constitution is a necessary basis for an economical administration . . .

I do not say, Sir, that all these establishments, whose principle is gone, have been systemmatically kept up for influence solely: neglect had its share. But this I am sure of: that a consideration of influence has hindered any one from attempting to pull them down. For the purposes of influence, and for those purposes only, are retained half at least of the household establishments. No revenue, no, not a royal revenue, can exist under the accumulated charge of ancient establishment, modern luxury, and Parliamentary political corruption . . .

All these incumbrances, which are themselves nuisances, produce other incumbrances and other nuisances. For the payment of these useless establishments there are no less than *three useless treasurers*: two to hold a purse, and one to play with a stick. The treasurer of the household is a mere name. The cofferer and the treasurer of the chamber receive and pay great sums, which it is not at all necessary *they* should either receive or pay. All the proper officers, servants, and tradesmen may be enrolled in their several departments, and paid in proper classes and times with great simplicity and order, at the Exchequer, and by direction from the Treasury . . .

By these regulations taken together, besides the three subordinate treasuries in the lesser principalities, five other subordinate treasuries are suppressed. There is taken away the whole *establishment of detail* in the household: the *treasurer*; the *comptroller* (for a comptroller is hardly necessary where there is no treasurer); the *cofferer of the household*; the *treasurer of the chamber*; the *master of the household*; the whole *board of green cloth*; — and a vast number of subordinate offices in the department of the *steward of the household*, — the whole establishment of the *great wardrobe*, — the *removing wardrobe*, — the *jewel office*, — the *robes*, — the *Board of Works*, — almost the whole charge of the *civil branch* of the *Board of Ordnance*, are taken away. All these arrangements together will be found to relieve the nation from a vast weight of influence, without distressing, but rather by forwarding every public service . . .

I know, too, that it will be demanded of me, how it comes, that, since I admit these offices [*the great patent offices in the Exchequer*] to be no better than pensions, I chose, after the principle of law had been satisfied, to retain them at all. To this, Sir, I answer, that, conceiving it to be a fundamental part of the Constitution of this country, and of the reason of state in every country, that there must be means of rewarding public service, those means will be incomplete, and indeed wholly insufficient for that purpose, if there should be no further reward for that service than the daily wages it receives during the pleasure of the crown . . . Indeed, no man knows, when he cuts off the incitements to a virtuous ambition, and the just rewards of public service, what infinite mischief he may do his country through all generations. Such saving to the public may prove the worst mode of robbing it. The crown, which has in its hands the trust of the daily pay for national service, ought to have in its hand also the means for the repose of public labor and the fixed settlement of acknowledged merit. There is a time when the weather-beaten vessels of the state ought to come into harbor . . .

I would therefore leave to the crown the possibility of conferring some favors, which, whilst they are received as a reward, do not operate as corruption . . .

I mean next to propose to you the *plan of arrangement*, by which I mean to appropriate and fix the civil list money to its several services according to their nature: for I am thoroughly sensible, that, if a discretion wholly arbitrary can be exercised over the civil list revenue, although the most effectual methods may be taken to prevent the inferior departments from exceeding their bounds, the plan of reformation will still be left very imperfect . . .

I am sensible, too, that the very operation of a plan of economy which tends to exonerate the civil list of expensive establishments may in some sort defeat the capital end we have in view — the independence of Parliament; and that, in removing the public and ostensible means of influence, we may increase the fund of private corruption . . .

The plan consists, indeed, of many parts; but they stand upon a few plain principles . . . It weakens no one function necessary to government; but on the contrary, by appropriating supply to service, it gives it greater vigor . . . It extinguishes secret corruption almost to the possibility of its existence. It destroys direct and visible influence equal to the offices of at least fifty members of Parliament . . . I pursue economy in a secondary view.

Speech on Presenting to the House of Commons a Plan for the Better Security of the Independence of Parliament . . . 11 February 1780, in *Works* (London, 1899), ii, 267-359.

11 The Establishment and Function of the Chief Government Departments in 1786, as Reported by Parliamentary Commissioners

The Establishment of the Secretary of State's Office in each Department consists of a Principal Secretary of State, two Under Secretaries, a Chief and other Clerks (ten in the Home, and nine in the Foreign Department) together with two Chamber Keepers, and a Necessary Woman.

To the Home Department is at present annexed a subordinate Office for Plantation Affairs, consisting of an Under Secretary and three Clerks. There are likewise attached generally to both Departments the Offices of a Gazette Writer, his Deputy, a Keeper of State Papers, a Collector and Transmitter of State Papers, two Commissioners for methodizing and digesting the State Papers, a Secretary for the Latin Language, two Decypherers, and sixteen Messengers.

The business of the Secretary of State's Office appears to consist in receiving intelligence, conducting correspondence, preparing and issuing warrants, and managing transactions relative to the Executive Government of the British Empire. Such of this business as relates to the British Dominions, and to the Four States of Barbary, is carried on in the Home Department, in which there is a subordinate Office for the Affairs of the Colonies. Such on the other hand as relates to the Foreign Powers of Europe, and the United States of America, is carried on in the Foreign Department.

The duty of the Principal Secretaries of State is to lay all such business before Your Majesty, to receive Your Majesty's commands thereupon, and to give the necessary orders accordingly to their respective Departments.

The duty of the Under Secretaries is to attend to the execution of such orders, to prepare drafts of such special letters and instructions, as occasion may require; to transact themselves whatever is of the most confidential nature; and

78

generally to superintend the business of the Office in all its branches.

The duty of the Chief Clerk is to distribute the ordinary official business among the Clerks; to see that all warrants and other instruments are duly prepared, transmitted to the proper persons for signature, and delivered to the respective parties, when application is made, and the regular Fees paid for the same; likewise, that the Office Books are properly kept, and the public Dispatches punctually transmitted. He further acts as the Accountant of the Office, in which capacity he receives and accounts for the Secretary of State's Salary, all the Fees and Gratuities, together with such other sums as are issued for defraying the general expense of the Office.

The remaining Clerks, who are distinguished by the rank of Senior and Junior in the Home Department, though without any such distinction in the Foreign, obey such orders as they receive from their superiors in office, but have no particular branches of business assigned to them.

The attendance of the efficient Under Secretaries is constant and unremitting: That of the Chief Clerks is likewise constant; and the other Clerks, though not always employed, are in daily attendance, and are expected to be ready for the execution of any business in which their superiors may think necessary to employ them.

The duty of the other inferior Officers is sufficiently expressed by the titles of their Offices, and is such as to occasion their constant attendance.

It remains to describe the duty of the officers attached generally to both Departments. The Offices of Gazette Writer, Keeper of State Papers, Collector and Transmitter of State Papers, and Secretary for the Latin Language, though they had each a duty originally annexed to them, obvious from their respective titles, are in their present state entirely Sinecures; and the Office of Deputy to the Gazette Writer is very nearly such, having no other duty than the insertion from time to time of official intelligence in the Gazette according to the form and precedent. The Commissioners for methodizing and digesting the State Papers having been put into possession of the Paper Office, with a view to the arrangement of the State Papers, continue to have the custody of the same, and execute at present the whole duties of the Keeper, and of the Collector and Transmitter: They receive and arrange all books and papers transmitted to them by authority from the Secretary of State's Offices, or otherwise; and obey such orders respecting the same, as they receive from Your Majesty or Your Principal Secretaries of State; and one of the Commissioners is in daily attendance for this purpose. The duty of the Decypherers is implied by their title, as is likewise that of the Messengers.

The Expenses of these Establishments are defrayed from various sources.

Out of Your Majesty's Civil List, there issues annually the sum of £640 in Patent Salaries, and £15,260 in Salaries at pleasure; also the Charges for Stationary and Incidents, which amounted in the year 1784 to £4,426.18.11½.

Out of the Post Office Revenue there issues the two several allowances granted by Parliament to the Clerks in the two Departments; the first consisting of £1,500 granted in the year 1769, in lieu of the privilege of franking letters generally; and the second of £1,000, granted in the year 1784, in lieu of the privilege of franking news-papers to Ireland . . .

From the East India Company there is received the annual present of Fifty Guineas, divided among the principal Clerks in the two Departments.

In Fees of Office there arises a considerable sum, which amounted in the year 1784 to £7,362.14.6; a fixed proportion of which goes to the Under Secretaries, Chief Clerks, and the Chamber Keepers in each Office. Out of the remainder, the Principal Secretaries pay the Clerk's salaries, and certain contingencies of Office, and retain the residue for their own use . . .

The official duty of the Under Secretaries of State appears to have been executed by one person in each Department. In the Home Department, one of the Under Secretaries was abroad with Your Majesty's leave at the time of making this Enquiry: and in the Foreign Department, one of these Offices never has been filled up since the present Secretary of State for that Department came into Office. It is therefore reasonable to conclude that for the necessary official business of each

Department, one Under Secretary is sufficient; and we are of opinion that for the obvious reason of preventing the confusion and serious consequences that may arise in business of such high importance, from frequent changes, such Officer ought to be made stationary . . .

From what we have been able to collect, the general business of the Office is scarcely sufficient to furnish full employment for the Clerks at present borne upon the establishment; and we consider their present number as rather to be justified by the propriety of having fit persons always in readiness upon any extraordinary pressure of business, than from the degree of employment which the Office ordinarily affords. If they were reduced to eight in each Department, your Majesty's service might not suffer from such reduction.

First Report of the Commissioners appointed . . . to enquire into the Fees, Gratuities, Perquisites, and Emoluments, which are or have been lately received in the several PUBLIC OFFICES, 11 April 1786, *Parliamentary Papers* HC 1806, vii (309), pp.3-10.

12 A Contemporary Commentary

GEORGE ROSE

Rose had been Pitt's patronage secretary. This pamphlet was based on a speech defending the use of patronage and was heavily attacked by Henry Brougham in the 'Edinburgh Review'. His argument, however, had a firm base: the government had lost many types of influence.

Of these topics of strict investigation there are particularly two, which Parliament in its inherent and necessary function is frequently called upon to examine and to discuss, on behalf of themselves and of their constituents — the *Influence of the Crown*, and the *Public Expenditure*; the last indeed as important with reference to the former, as from its own substantive effects on the ease and happiness of the people. Its importance, in both points of view, is in proportion to its magnitude; and now, therefore, when the circumstances of the times, and the situation of the country, call for its exertion beyond all former example, almost beyond all former conjecture, it is doubly incumbent on the House of Commons to exercise that guardianship of the public purse with which it is invested, by increasing checks, and by frequent enquiry.

This part of its duty, Parliament has, in fact, performed within the last four-and-twenty years in a manner more efficient, as well as more active, than at any former period of our political history . . .

Besides the general construction (if the phrase may be allowed) of our government, adapted at all times to the purpose of checking excess as well as abuse in its expenditure, there should be an occasional adoption of enquiry to suit particular cases and particular departments. This mode is rendered indispensible from the complication as well as the novelty, of many articles of public expense to which important and critical periods give rise; in addition to which there is also an energy in newly established institutions for restraint or investigation beyond the customary routine of official supervision. In the superintendance of great and widely extended concerns, no vigilance of department can at all times guard against possible abuses; frauds, or culpable negligence, will occasionally escape the detection of ordinary management, notwithstanding the utmost circumspection of vigilant officers. The best chance of discovering such particular abuses, or of suggesting general improvements in future, will be found in special enquiries from time to time . . . This pointed exercise of enquiry is now become so much a political habit in this country, that we may venture to trust no future administration will discountenance it, nor any future generation allow it to go into disuse.

The precedents and practice of such useful enquiries, like the precedents and practice of all other great public institutions, it is extremely important should be unfolded and illustrated. It is with an intention to a discharge of that duty to the country, that the following accurate statement of the measures which have been already adopted towards the attainment of the objects above alluded to, in one point of view, is made; so as not only to shew what has been done towards retrenchment of the public expence, and the consequent diminution of the patronage of the crown, but also to exhibit the present subsisting state of such expence and patronage so much in detail, as to afford every person the means of judging what further retrenchments may reasonably be expected, consistently with the good of the public service, and, what in truth is synonimous, with proper encouragement and reward of merit in the servants of the public.

	No. of Offices	Annual Value
By the Civil List Act, brought in by Mr Burke in 1782, 22 Geo.3.c.82 there were actually suppressed	134	57,500
Under regulations of the Treasury in 1782-3, by Lord Shelburne and Mr Pitt	144	13,625
Making a total of offices in the Civil List, suppressed in 1782-3, of	278	71,125
But there were offices created to perform the duties of those suppressed, to the amount of	62	10,909
Making a reduction at that time in the Civil List, on the whole, of	216	£60,216
The Exchequer Act in 1783, the 23 Geo.3.c.82. *suppressed* the Usher, Tally Cutters, the two Chamberlains, and the four Second Clerks in The Tellers Offices, all valuable sinecures; but these suppressions were not to fall in till the deaths of the parties	8	10,000
Under the same act, the offices of Auditor and four Tellers were *regulated*, to take effect after the deaths of the then possessors; the income of the former was at that time £19,800 a year, and would have been more now than is here stated, at		60,000
The four Tellers would now have been		88,000
Suppressions and regulations in the Exchequer		158,000
Deduct the salaries of the Auditor and of the four Tellers		14,800
Actual saving in the department of the Exchequer		143,200

	No. of Offices	Annual Value
The Auditors' act in 1785, 25 Geo.3. c.52. suppressed offices, the fees of which, on the National Debt alone at £100 a million, would now have amounted to more than £60,000 a year, on the accompts of the Bank, &c. and therefore on the whole of the public accounts audited by those officers may be moderately stated at		70,000
From which must be deducted as under,		
Expense of all sorts of the New Board, in 1785,	9,900	
Additions in 1801,	10,032	
Between 1801 and 1805,	850	
In 1805, a new Board was constituted of three Commissioners and Officers	9,575	
And in 1806, the two Boards were consolidated, two Commissioners added, with an increased establishment, amounting in the whole to	14,811	
Total of the present establishment of auditing public accounts		*45,168
Actual saving of charge in this department		24,832

The increased charge, occasioned by the immense accumulation of public accompts, has prevented the direct saving by the above-mentioned measure being considerable; but the positive advantages derived to the country from the strict investigation, which those accounts have undergone since 1785, are of incalculable value. The number of employments were not altered by the suppression of the two Auditors of the imprest under the Act in that year, and the subsequent suppression

*From this however should be deducted the salary of one Commissioner who is dead, to whom no successor is to be appointed.

	No. of Offices	Annual Value
of the Auditorship of hides, as three Commissioners were added to the two existing Comptrollers of Army accompts, to constitute the new Board then established. The subsequent acts added seven Commissioners, making the whole number ten,* without the Comptrollers, who ceased to be auditors under the last act, and one was added to their number; but the office of one of the new auditors having lapsed by death, and not being to be filled up, the increase in this department on the whole to be deducted is	7	
Diminution in the number of employments, and saving in the annual charge in the Civil List and the Exchequer	217 Offices	
Of the annual value of —	—	£228,248

Nothing can be more remote from the intention of the present publication, than a wish to discourage enquiry, or to prevent the suggestion of salutary checks: the real object of it is to lead others to examine the ground on which the necessity of adopting stronger measures of restraint as well as of investigation, at the present period, has been repeatedly urged, frequently with the best intentions, and with the purest motives . . .

The amount of sinecure employments cannot be compared with former periods, as there are no means for enabling that to be done; but we shall find the amount of pensions occasionally in the Journals. In the last year of Queen Anne, it was £130,000 nett in England only, as the 1s. and 6d. taxes did not then

*When the Act was depending in the House of Commons in 1806, the Author ventured to express an opinion, that increasing the number of Commissioners would rather retard than accelerate the examination of the public accompts; instead of which increase he proposed the addition of some more inspectors. Experience may now be resorted to, to decide whether that opinion was well founded.

exist . . . The opinion already alluded to, as prevailing to a certain extent, that if sinecures and pensions were entirely suppressed, the burthens of the country would be instantly lightened to a great amount, and by some entertained, that they would, in that case, be removed altogether, renders it necessary that a comparison should be made of the before-mentioned total, large as it is, with the amount of the taxes raised upon the people.

The whole revenue of Great Britain is more than £60,000,000 a-year; the charge on which of £242,000, for pensions and sinecure employments at home and abroad, is between three farthings and one penny in the pound. By the extinction, therefore, of all sinecures and pensions, a person paying taxes to the amount of £50 a-year would save about 4s. Such a saving we are far from thinking should be treated as trifling or insignificant; it would ill become the author to do so: on the other hand, how infinitely short would this fall of the expectation that has been held out?

But if from the total sum received from sinecure places and pensions, deductions were made of such as have been given as rewards for public services, the amount would be very greatly reduced; pensions to foreign ministers, in particular, whose appointments are hardly, in any instance, sufficient for their maintenance.

The pension list also contains provision for the branches of noble and respectable families fallen into decay; this is however an exertion of national generosity, if not of justice, which the most scrupulous economist will hardly consider as improper. Something must certainly be allowed for mere favor; but when the instances are clearly improper (and it is not meant to contend there are no such), they are at least open to public animadversion; as they are now regularly laid before parliament, and printed from time to time, which certainly affords a considerable, if not an effectual, check against abuse.

If we look to official incomes, it will be found they are, in most cases, barely equal to the moderate, and even the necessary expences of the parties; in many instances they are actually insufficient for these. May we not then venture to ask, whether it is reasonable, or whether it would be politic, that such persons should, after spending a great part of their lives with industry, zeal and fidelity, in the discharge of trusts and public duties, be left afterwards without reward of any sort, and their families entirely without provision?

It would hardly be wise, on reflection, to establish a principle which would have a tendency at least to exclude from the service of their country Men likely to be useful to it. Great numbers of those who engage in trade and manufacture (than whom none are held in higher estimation by the author) or who enter into various professions, frequently acquire very large fortunes, and seldom, if they have talents and perseverance, fail to obtain independence. What fairness, justice, or reason is there then in marking the character of the official man alone with disrespect, and himself as unfit to have reward in any case, beyond an annual stipend for his labour and services, just sufficient for his necessary current expences, however faithfully and diligently he may have discharged an important trust for a long series of years? Surely it is not unwise or unreasonable that the public should be in a situation to bid to a limited extent for talents, in competition with other honourable and lucrative professions, and various branches of trade and manufactures . . .

The retrenchments which have been suggested on more sober grounds, though occasionally by persons not the most conversant either with the resources or the necessary expenditure of the state, have been of two kinds; either of mere economy, supposing the services to be indispensable; or of policy, supposing the services to be needless. The last, it is obvious, ought at all times to be weighed carefully; and with a sober and deliberate judgment . . . no new or additional expence should be incurred in any department, without the previous knowledge and entire approbation of the minister, who is responsible for the due management of the finances of the country, and for keeping down the expenditure in every department . . . but above all in times like the present, when our war-establishment of every fort is not only the instrument of our national glory, but the means of our national safety, the provision for our national existence. The other branch of saving, that by which the same services may be performed at a cheaper rate, deserves the most serious investigation, and, it is hoped, has undergone the most anxious consideration, in order to the attainment of that laudable end. But the retrenchments should leave the substantial objects of the expenditure in as full efficient vigour as before; otherwise the safety of the country would be endangered, at a moment when the storm beats furiously against it, and the ruins of other political fabrics are seen all around us . . .

The greatly increased revenue, and all the other augmented and accumulated business of the state have unavoidably occasioned some increase of patronage; but the influence created by such means is infinitely short of what has been given up by the measures of economy and regulation to which recourse has been had, especially when the description and value of the employments created is compared with those abolished; and it will not be denied to us that the manners of the times; the constant existence of a watchful opposition; the modern usage of parliament; the liberty of the press; and the unbounded circulation of the productions which that liberty encourages; all conspire to limit in practice that influence which, in other times, was so powerful and so prevailing . . . there has not been a reign in which the influence of the Crown has been so unceasingly controlled by the jealousy of the House of Commons as that of His present Majesty.

Observations respecting the Public Expenditure and the Influence of the Crown, (London, 1810), pp.2-8, 60-5, 73-6.

13 The 'Influence' of the Crown

ARCHIBALD S. FOORD

Now, on the one hand, it is clearly established that the influence of the crown was not destroyed in 1782. The myth concerning George III's loss of power during Pitt's ministries has been dispelled, and no legislation prevented the most effective use of crown influence to secure a government majority in the election of 1784. Moreover, the economical reforms of the Rockinghamites, though they achieved a moderate diminution of the 'king's interest', fell far short of the goal, and the reforms were so imperfectly conceived that much further legislation was required.

On the other hand, there is considerable evidence which indicates that the old system of making and controlling majorities had been broken before 1832 . . . As early as 1809, Thomas Grenville pointed out that 'the influence of what they call corruption is, for practical purposes, too small rather than too great', though he added that this could not be said in public.

After 1780 . . . legislation and administrative reorganisation inexorably broke up the old system of patronage. Here the same forces were at work which effected a reduction in both 'imperceptible influence' and the pecuniary influence of the crown, and a changing attitude toward the employment of patronage worked in the same direction. A comparison of the situation in the disposal of patronage in several of the most important fields before and after 1780 will indicate the nature of the great alterations which took place.

Sinecure offices, once termed by Castlereagh 'more likely than any others to secure parliamentary influence', had played a considerable part before 1780 in attaching ministerial adherents . . . Although no move was made to weed out such functionless offices until the second Rockingham ministry, in 1782 there commenced a constant and unremitting attack upon sinecures. Burke's Act abolished 134 offices in household and ministry. Treasury regulations under Shelburne did away with 144 sinecures in the customs, and the Exchequer Act of 1783 condemned a large number of exchequer sinecures to extinction upon the death of their incumbents. George Rose estimated that Pitt's reforms abolished 765 needless revenue offices in 1789 and another 196 in 1798. Legislation in the early nineteenth century weeded out still more useless offices, many of which had been converted into sinecures by administrative reform. A select committee of the commons, appointed to investigate sinecures from 1810 to 1812, found that many of the 342 sinecures still existing were to be abolished upon the death of their holders. Another investigation in 1817 resulted in the abolition or 'regulation' of 313 other useless offices. In 1822 Castlereagh boasted that since 1815 more than 2000 civil offices rendered useless by the close of the war had been abolished . . .

The destruction of the sinecure accompanied that of the old method of granting offices in reversion. When demands for patronage were greater than the supply, the government had sometimes promised offices upon the death or removal of the incumbent . . . But acts regulating sinecures commonly prohibited grants in reversion, and an Act of 1808 which temporarily suspended the power to grant any office in this way was later extended through 1814. Thereafter the use of reversions as a means of influence fell into desuetude.

Another great change in the system of patronage occurred in the revenue departments. Before 1780 the treasury had engrossed all appointments in customs and excise, and the numerous revenue officers had been turned into borough voters and electioneers for the ministry of the day . . . The revenue officer, more than any other factor, produced the 'treasury boroughs' of the eighteenth century. In 1782, however, Crewe's Act disfranchised the majority of revenue officers . . . After the union with Ireland, disfranchisement was extended to Irish revenue officers, and henceforward the placeman-voter ceased to exist as a widespread institution. The development of preliminary qualifications for civil servants from 1787 onwards also worked to remove political influence from revenue appointments.

In other spheres the patronage system was weakened not by legislation but by custom . . . Walpole once roundly declared that if any officer should 'even show aversion to a minister, that minister would be the most wretched of creatures if he did not cashier him, and he left the practice as a legacy to his successors' . . . Lords lieutenant were treated in the same fashion . . . Early in the nineteenth century this practice came to an end . . . The ministry still possessed the unquestioned right to cashier such opponents, but declined to continue political patronage in the army and county government.

There are evidences of similar if less emphatic trends in appointments to the church, the law, and the colonies.

This evidence of a decline in the resources of crown influence lends considerable weight to the plaints of politicians in the reign of George IV that the old system of government 'corruption' was then breaking up . . .

A particular moment in time when the influence of the crown became insufficient to control parliament cannot be definitely determined . . . The destruction of the influence of the crown occurred, not in the 1780's nor in 1832, but in the period lying between. It was effected, not by any enactment or group of enactments, but by a long train of legislation, administrative reform, and changed attitudes in public life. The forces motivating these alterations were the constant pressure of opposition parties striving to reduce ministerial power, the need for economy and retrenchment after the American revolution and during and after the wars of the French revolution, and the social and economic changes in British life as reflected in the growth of the power of public opinion through a cheaper and more influential press.

'The waning of "The influence of the Crown" ', *English Historical Review*, lxii, (1947), 486-7, 499-507.

14 The Civil Service

(a) HENRY PARRIS

When did the permanent civil service come into being? . . . Without some such reservation, the use of the term in relation to periods earlier than the half-century 1780-1830 is an obstacle to understanding. The 'permanent civil service' prior to that time differed from its modern counterpart in three significant ways. It was not permanent, it was not civil, and it was not a service . . . The expression 'a service' implies a body of full-time, salaried officers, systematically recruited, with clear lines of authority, and uniform rules on such questions as superannuation. These conditions did not exist in the eighteenth century . . .

The development of administration as an autonomous sphere, distinct from politics, in the period 1780-1830 had three important aspects. First, the non-military servants of the Crown began to develop into a service . . . Typical of the steps taken were the abolition of patent offices, payment of salaries (under Treasury control) instead of fees, and the introduction of superannuation (again under Treasury control).

Secondly, members of this nascent service came to be known as civil — i.e. non-political — servants of the Crown. The term 'civil servant' was first used in India in contrast to the military servants of the East India Company. When first used in Britain it had a similar sense; for example, in Palmerston's memorandum on relations between the Secretary at War and the Commander in Chief, dated 1811, where he speaks of the former as 'a civil servant of the Crown' . . . What appears to be the earliest document to embody the modern distinction is a Treasury circular, probably dating from 1816, which speaks of 'servants in the Civil Service of the country' and so eligible for superannuation as distinct from political servants, who were not.

Thirdly, and most importantly, the emergent civil service had become permanent . . . The process was more or less complete by 1830. The administrative factors involved were, firstly, the increasing bulk of departmental business and, secondly, its increasing complexity . . . It was the middle level — the sub-ministers, the under-secretaries — who bore the brunt . . .

Probably the War Office was the first department to have an official corresponding in function with the modern permanent secretary . . . The Post Office was not far behind.

In the offices of the three Secretaries of State, there were six Under Secretaries. As late as 1806, they were liable to change on a change of government, though those in the rank immediately below (the chief clerks) were by that time held to be permanent officers.

Constitutional Bureaucracy (Allen and Unwin, 1969), pp.21-43.

(b) HENRY ROSEVEARE

Clearly Burke had penetrated the two fundamental anomalies which had debilitated eighteenth-century government — the doctrinaire divorce between the legislature and the civil executive, and the lack of any responsible, centralized administrative control. The remedies he offered — piecemeal economies in the Civil List, the Exchequer and the great spending departments — do not quite seem to match up to the profundity of his diagnosis, and Burke's actual achievement fell far short of his vision, but he has the considerable merit of having pointed in the right direction and of having broken the spell which had so far paralysed the constitution.

The Treasury Reform of 1782

. . . The commendable aspects of this reform are fairly clear. The yoking together of senior and junior clerks in a Division enhanced the educational possibilities of specialization, and improved the chances of administrative continuity. The range of Treasury business was not wide enough to permit a functional distribution of business without depriving the Divisions of a balanced diet. Thus, most of them superintended a branch of revenue, all dealt with expenditure and all controlled establishments on the Civil List. But each Division — the Third with Army and Navy business, the Fifth with Customs and Excise — had some solid core of responsibility round which it revolved.

Unhappily, anomalies survived. The clerks received the traditional New Year gifts from their principal clients in varying amounts which were sometimes large enough to upset the seniority scale. Pluralism among Treasury clerks was to survive for another fifty years. Recruitment was not improved and few promotions flouted the claims of seniority. In other words, the Treasury remained a pleasant haven for gentlemen of good connections and modest abilities, jogging along in the comparative comfort of an assured income and regular hours.

The Treasury (Allen Lane, 1969), pp.121-3.

(c) SINECURE OFFICES IN 1810
SELECT COMMITTEE REPORT

A Select Committee was appointed in 1810 to pursue the problem of sinecure offices and divided public offices into four categories which they felt to be in need of reform.

1. Offices having Revenue without Employment;
2. Offices having Revenue extremely disproportionate to Employment; and,
3. Offices of which the effective duties are entirely or principally discharged by a Deputy. [Excepting always such Offices as are connected with the personal service of His Majesty, or of His Royal Family.]
4. Offices, the appointments to which are allowed to be sold in any of the Courts of Law.

Your Committee have to observe, that the number of Offices which have Revenue without any Employment, either of Principal or Deputy, is very inconsiderable; and that by far the greatest number of Offices which are commonly described as "Sinecure Offices" fall properly under the description "Offices executed by Deputy", or "Offices having Revenue disproportionate to Employment".

Among the Offices, the Revenue of which appears disproportionate to Employment, or which are performed principally by Deputy, there are some to which great pecuniary and official responsibility is attached; and some, from the holders of which large securities are required. It may therefore be expedient that such Offices should not at any time be filled by persons less responsible than those who at present hold them.

In other cases it seems probable that the Principals may, under peculiar circumstances, have provided for the discharge of their duties by Deputy at a lower salary than that which might fairly be considered as an adequate remuneration for the services to be performed, and which might, indeed, be necessary to ensure the due performance of those services, should it be found expedient to withdraw the superintendence and authority of the Principal.

It appears therefore to Your Committee, that in some

instances it might be expedient to annex the duties of such of the Offices to be regulated, as have great responsibility, without requiring continual personal attendance, to other Offices of an efficient nature; by which means a saving of the whole Revenue of such regulated Offices might accrue to the Public, while sufficient provision would be made for the responsibility of the person in whom they may hereafter be vested.

Parliamentary Papers, HC 1810, ii, 591-2, (362), pp. 1-2.

15 The Confusions of Local Government

At a local level, variety of form and levels of efficiency was everywhere to be found. The parish remained the basic administrative unit and the Justices of the Peace the local executive officers in both town and countryside.

(a) THE PARISH OF
ST GEORGE, HANOVER SQUARE, WESTMINSTER

Three or more governors and directors may act, and make rules and orders.

One overseer to be appointed for each ward in the parish.

Power to enlarge the infirmary, and build a chapel, and purchase places for employing the poor; and to borrow money for those purposes: £10,000 at interest, and 5 per cent yearly to be paid off . . .

Power to hire places to employ the poor, and to keep the workhouse and other buildings in repair . . .

Vestry may appoint surveyors of the highways.

Rate to be laid for the relief of the poor, and for repairing highways . . .

Vestry to appoint beadles, watchmen, and patrols . . .

Vestry to appoint a committee for paving, cleansing, and lighting the streets . . . Committee to cause the streets to be repaired, cleansed, and lighted, and the garden in Hanover Square to be embellished . . . Names of streets to be put up, and houses and lamp-irons numbered . . .

Rates not to exceed the highest sum raised in any year within the last six years . . .

Number of vestrymen to constitute a meeting, of the rector, or curate, and one churchwarden, and eight vestrymen . . .

Statutes at Large, xlii (1789), pp.812-13.

(b) THE STAFF OF
THE JUSTICE OF THE PEACE

Permanent and salaried officials were not unknown of course in local government for the local Justices had for long relied upon the clerical and administrative help of the deputy clerk of the peace. The Clerk of the Peace himself, an appointment in the hands of the *custos rotulorum*, was generally a gentleman or a man of means who appointed a local attorney in his place . . .

The office of treasurer was instituted in most counties in the early years of the eighteenth century, but it was at first rather casual and haphazard in character . . .

That other salaried officer, the county surveyor, was even slower to appear. Though the county was being forcibly reminded in the matter of prisons of its responsibilities for such rudimentary public services it was only with the greatest reluctance that the Justices were willing to admit the necessity of a permanent and professional skilled architect or engineer in the place of their old habit of farming out jobs as they came up to some small bricklayer or carpenter . . . Buckinghamshire had a salaried surveyor of bridges from 1804 to 1822, but then appointed no successor until 1838. Perhaps underlying this was the feeling that any country gentleman who possessed sufficient knowledge of the techniques of building, drainage and engineering to run his estates could by the same token take adequate care of his locality.

E. Moir, *The Justice of the Peace* (Penguin, 1969), pp.116-118.

III

Signs of Change: the 1830s

After the 'economical reform' movement of the 1780s, Parliament instigated a succession of enquiries into the spending of public money. These enquiries continued well into the nineteenth century and covered virtually every aspect of salaries and emoluments in the public service. Slowly it became apparent that the chief aim of the reformers was that of economy. While criticism of the use of sinecures and places for political ends continued, the dramatic increase in taxation as a result of the Napoleonic Wars ensured ready support for the cry of retrenchment so often heard in the Commons in the 1830s.

16 Sinecure Offices in 1834

A SELECT COMMITTEE REPORT

In reviewing the remaining offices included in the Returns referred to them, Your Committee have proceeded in the firm persuasion that anything in the nature of a Sinecure Office, with emoluments attached to it at the public charge, is alike indefensible in principle, pernicious as a means of influence, and grievous as an undue addition to the general burthens of the Nation. They assume with confidence that it is the anxious wish of The House, in discharge of its obligations to the Country, and in conformity with the feeling of the Public, to extinguish altogether this objectionable class of offices as early as may be practicable, consistent with a just regard to all legitimate claims and interests of the present holders.

Conformably with these views, Your Committee have turned their attention to ascertain with respect to each individual office, first, under what tenure it is now held by the present possessor, whether by grant for his life, or by grant during good behaviour, or by grant during pleasure of the Crown; next, whether any Act of Parliament has been passed, prospectively abolishing the office, or prospectively regulating it, so as to preclude the possibility of its being re-granted as a Sinecure to any new holder . . .

The following offices included in the annexed Return are held as Sinecures by patent during the pleasure of the Crown.

No.51 — Inspector General of Coffee and Tea.
   73 — King's Almoner in *Scotland*.
   75 — Housekeepers of Dublin Castle.
   94 — Register of Forfeitures (*Ireland*).
   95 — Physician to the State.

To which Your Committee have to add, though it is not included in the annexed Returns, the office of Receiver of First Fruits and Tenths, an office executed wholly by deputy . . .

Your Committee recommend, that this latter class of offices should be forthwith abolished, and the patents to the existing holders revoked; provision being made for the discharge of any duty annexed to any of the said offices, wherever such duty is now performed by deputy . . .

Your Committee find, that the Keeper of the Great Seal in Scotland, discharging no duties in person, receives fees to the amount of £1,024, paying to his deputy for the discharge of the duties annexed to the office, the sum of £600. Besides the clear surplus of fees now received by the Keeper of the Great Seal, there was formerly a salary of £2,000 per annum annexed to the office, which was discontinued in the year 1831, at the recommendation of the Committee of the House of Commons in that year on the subject of Salaries. Your Committee are unable to understand why the same principles which induced a former Committee to recommend the discontinuance of the salary annexed to this office, should not also be extended to the other emoluments received by the Keeper of the Great Seal, in the form of a clear surplus of fees. They think that the Treasury ought to make this office a subject of special investigation, with a view to ensure ultimately the transfer of this surplus to the Consolidated Fund, reserving only what may be sufficient for the remuneration of the deputy, by whom the entire duties of the office are discharged.

The following offices are held as Sinecures under patent grants for the life of the holder, or during good behaviour, without any legislative provision having yet been made for prospectively regulating or abolishing them.

No. 33 —⎱ Register Writer of the Prero-
36 —⎰ gative Court, and Clerks of the Seat.
38 — Prothonotary of the Palace Court.
28 — Messengers of the Court of Exchequer.
39 — Collector of State Papers.
44 — Clerk of the Privy Seal.
54 — Surveyor of Plantations.
69 — Principal Clerk of Justiciary (*Scotland*).
80 — Second Remembrancer of the Exchequer
81 — Registrar of the Prerogative Court
82 — Marshal of the Prerogative Court   *Ireland*
92 — Clerk of the Pipe
89 — Usher of the Court of Chancery Governor of the Isle of Wight.

It is the opinion of Your Committee, that provision ought to be made forthwith, by Act of Parliament, for the prospective regulation or abolition of all these offices, so as to preclude the future appointment of any new individuals as sinecure holders of them, either by the Crown or by any other parties in whom such right of appointment may now reside . . .

It is a point of considerable importance, in the view of Your Committee, that the Treasury should lay before Parliament, in the course of the ensuing Session, an account of all steps which they may then have taken, to carry into effect the recommendations of the present Report. The Public will thus have increased assurance, that no unnecessary delay shall take place in rectifying so much of the abuse of Sinecure Offices as is open to immediate economical regulation . . .

Your Committee have been anxious to lay before The House a statement of the amount of charge now incurred by the Public from the salaries and emoluments of existing Sinecures, as compared with former periods.

On consulting the Report of the Select Committee on Sinecure Offices appointed in 1810, they find that in that year, according to the Papers referred to that Committee, there were in existence throughout His Majesty's Dominions 242 offices which, according to the opinion of that Committee, came under the denomination of Sinecures, and of which the total net income amounted to £297,095 per annum.

By the Return of the Sinecure Offices now in existence referred to Your Committee, it appears that there remain 100 offices of a similar description, the total net emoluments of which amount to £97,803.

Your Committee have prepared the following Table, which will show the progress which has been made in the abolition of Sinecures.

	1810		1834	
	AMOUNT of Emolument of existing Sinecures	AMOUNT of Prospective Saving by Abolition &c. provided for	AMOUNT of Emoluments of existing Sinecures	AMOUNT of Prospective Saving by Abolition &c. provided for
	£	£	£	£
England*	178,051	71,985	63,968	56,648
Scotland	25,000	—†	14,833	14,368
Ireland	76,435	16,362	19,002	19,968
TOTAL £	279,486	88,347	97,803	81,984

*Exclusive of Colonial Sinecures, of which the Committee have not yet examined the Return, the amount of which, in 1810, is stated at £17,000.
†Not distinguished.

The House will perceive from this Table, that the amount of Sinecures, for the ultimate abolition of which no Parliamentary enactment has provided, is already reduced from nearly £200,000 per annum, as it stood in 1810, to less than £17,000 per annum.

It is not in the power of Your Committee to give any sufficiently accurate account of the amount of pecuniary saving which has already accrued to the Public by the abolition of

Sinecures. Many offices which existed formerly as Sinecures, have been converted into, or united with, efficient offices; in some cases with, and in others without, a reduction of emolument. In most instances the abolition of an office, when immediate, has been accompanied by a compensation or allowance to the holder; in other cases the abolition has been prospective only, leaving the office itself to subsist until the determination of existing interests. The period, however, cannot be far distant, when by the natural expiration of these existing interests, the Country will reap the full benefit (either by the acquisition of effective services or by pecuniary saving) of those successive efforts which, from 1782 downwards, have operated in gradually disencumbering the finances of the Country from the justly obnoxious pressure of Sinecure emoluments.

Select Committee Report . . . respecting Sinecure Offices, *Parliamentary Papers*, HC 1834 vi, 339-48, (519), pp.3-10.

17 The Role of Individuals and Pressure Groups

Pressure on government departments and ministers for financial and administrative reform built up in the 1820s and 1830s. Two men in particular, Joseph Hume and Sir Henry Parnell, ensured that the pressure could not be resisted. In the field of social reform Richard Oastler and Edwin Chadwick dominated the Factory Acts and the new Poor Law respectively, both in their passing and execution.

(a) JOSEPH HUME

Hume harassed the Treasury in the Commons. Maintaining a private staff of clerks, he was able to challenge virtually every detail in the Estimates. His terrier-like qualities proved in general effective at least in eliciting detailed accounts from reluctant ministers. His persistence, however, also aroused resentment among officials and occasionally embarrassed his radical colleagues.

Mr *Hume* had never stated, that the present Ministry had made no reductions in the expenditure. On the contrary he knew, and had always said, that considerable reductions had been made, but that these reductions had not been commensurate with the wants of the country, or the wishes of the people. With respect to what the hon. Member for Coventry had said about the difficulty of making up the proofs of a financial statement, he wished to observe that since he had given the hon. Member that warning, things had considerably changed. He was happy to say, that a considerable simplification in the statement of public accounts had taken place since 1821. A Committee of Public Accounts had been appointed by Lord Bexley, in consequence of his recommendation; and now any one might make himself acquainted with the Finance Accounts without any such labour as formerly. Indeed, there would be now no difficulty in the matter, save and except so far as related to the sums stopped in their course to the Exchequer. The Civil List Accounts had also been simplified by his right hon. friend, but much yet remained to be done, and he trusted that all the accounts would be still further simplified, as they might be with little trouble, in the course of next year. He was sorry, however, to be obliged to tell his hon. friend that, after all the reductions which had been effected by the Government, they had only just left the expenditure at the level at which he found it when he took up this subject in 1821. The expenditure of 1833 was within a very small fraction as large as the expenditure of 1820. The reduction in the amount of it arose entirely from the diminished charge of the national debt since that time . . . In the year 1821 the expenditure was £53,000,000; now it was £50,000,000. Of this sum £28,000,000 and upwards went to pay the interest of the debt, so that the difference in the amount of the charge of the debt in 1819, and in 1823, was in round numbers, £2,900,000. Now this was, within a very small fraction, the sum of the difference between the amount of the expenditure in 1819 and in 1833. He, therefore, contended that he had a right to say, that the difference in the expenditure of the two years arose from the diminished charge of the national debt, effected as everybody knew, by the reduction of the £4 and the £5 per cent to stock bearing a lower rate of interest. The saving on the establishments of the year 1820 was now, in the year 1833, not more than £100,000. He admitted that in that interim the expenses of our establishments had much increased, and that the late Government had done much, and that the present Government had done more, to reduce our expenditure to the level of 1820. One great advantage had been derived to the country from the accession of the present Ministers to office, and that was, that they had reduced the charges on the Civil List, and had brought all the expenses of the State, save about half a million, under the control of Parliament. There was no department into which the House could not at present inquire, nor had any accounts for which he had moved yet been refused to his Motion. Happen what would, the House was now placed in a situation in which, with a little trouble, it could have the amplest statement of the national finances that man could wish . . . The point which he wished to bring the House to was this — that though Government had made great reductions, and though several of their changes in taxation had been very beneficial, the same amount as before was taken out of the pockets of the people. Now, he should wish to see the excise taken off all excisable articles; he should also wish to see the duties removed from all raw materials, as such duties were positive impediments to industry; he should wish to see all monopolies extinguished, and particularly the Corn monopoly, because he was convinced that if those beneficial changes were made, the country could bear its burthens with comparatively little trouble. He thought, that where a Government had made a profligate grant, and where it had allowed a man money for which he had performed no service, the same distinction ought to be drawn by Parliament, which, in a similar case, would be drawn by individuals in private life. Parliament ought, he contended, to look at every pension, and to stop the issue of every farthing of public money which was not merited by public service . . . He maintained against his hon. friend, that all sinecures ought to be swept away. He held, likewise, that the present Parliament had a right to abolish the pensions which were granted under the authority of a former Parliament . . . The time was fast advancing, and even now was arrived, when an inquiry into the circumstances under which every pension and every sinecure was granted, must take place . . . He cared not for the rank of the parties; the higher they were the more strict should be the investigation; the more means they had at command, the less regard should be paid to their complaints and remonstrances . . .

Hansard, third series, xix, 694-8, 16 July 1833.

(b) SIR HENRY PARNELL

Although associated with Joseph Hume, Parnell achieved office and maintained his campaign for economical reform both in and out of office. When the office of Paymaster-General of the Forces was reformed in 1836, he was appointed to it. His pamphlet 'On Financial Reform' which was aimed at the establishment of firm Treasury control of government spending was to bear fruit in the financial reforms of the 1850s and 1860s.

As the Treasury exercise the same powers, and discharge nearly the same duties now as they did in 1797, this immense increase of expense in the establishment of a department whose duty it is to control the other departments, is alone sufficient evidence of the profusion with which salaries must have been increased, and officers multiplied. There are no fewer than fifteen clerks in the Treasury, who receive salaries amounting to £1000; five of these fifteen receive £1500 a year each, and upwards.

Nothing can more fully shew the want of system and uniformity on the part of those persons by whom public business has been originally regulated, and the necessity of revision and reform, than the mode by which the Treasury establishment is paid — for instance, some of the salaries are paid out of the Civil List; some out of a fee-fund; some out of the Customs' revenue, and some by an annual grant of Parliament. Such kind of complication must lead to great perplexity and confusion of accounts, and frustrate all efforts to keep down the expense of official establishments . . .

The more the question of salaries is examined, the more fully it can be shewn that high salaries are not only the source of a great burden on the public, but also that they actually contribute to make the clerks less efficient, and, consequently, to the employing of a greater number of them. There cannot be a greater mistake than the notion generally entertained, that fitness will follow in proportion as the amount of the salary is high. Those persons who are willing to work for a small remuneration always have the greatest relish for work; and therefore, giving low salaries will secure the filling of the offices with the most efficient clerks. On the other hand, when a clerk has a high salary, the less will be his activity, and he will be wholly adverse to anything like the drudgery of office. He will possess a greater facility for enjoying pleasurable and other trivial occupations. He will have a greater facility of obtaining accomplices in his transgressions, and in finding supporters to shield him against being displaced, and against having his conduct thought disreputable.

The present rates of salaries of officers and clerks place them in a much better situation than the remuneration given to that part of the clergy, who perform the laborious part of the church duties, and to officers of high rank in the army and navy.

As the great pretext for raising all salaries to their present rates was the depreciation of money, now that the value of it is restored, the public have a right to require a reduction to be generally made on a large scale.

As it appears from a Paper laid before the House of Commons, that the sum paid for salaries in 1827 amounted to £2,788,907, such a rate of reduction would produce a considerable saving.

The Committee of Finance, in their Third Report, have pointed out the practicability of making a considerable retrenchment by means of a reform in the existing system of superannuation allowances. Since 1810, when the present law was passed, the charge for civil superannuations has increased from £94,550 to £480,081. The Committee say this increase is enormous, and represent it as an evil that calls loudly for a remedy. They state that several abuses have arisen under the law as it now is, particularly from the disposition of the superior authorities to favour the retirement of efficient clerks; they say they have been informed, that the cases are not few, in which persons superannuated as unfit for public service, have enjoyed health and strength long afterwards, and have discharged active duties in other public offices, and in private business; and they recommend that there should be a percentage reduction of all salaries, to form a fund for paying the superannuation allowances.

Nothing can be more extravagant, and inconsistent with a proper guardianship of the public money, than the system of salaries and superannuations now in operation. The salaries are so much higher than they ought to be, that every officer and clerk has more than means of making a provision for infirmity and old age. But notwithstanding this fact, as to the sufficiency of salary, in the true spirit of profusion, a great superannuation allowance has been added. If the Committee of Finance had decided in favour of what was most proper to be done in the case, they would have recommended the abolition of all such allowances on future appointment to office: for, although it might be difficult for Government to resist the claims of hardship and real sufferings, which would, in that event, be made upon them, it may be considered as quite certain that in their hands, the sums which would be granted would never amount to what is now paid under the compulsory plan of giving to every officer a regulated allowance. It is quite impossible to explain why we are to have a privileged class in society who, because they have once touched public money, are to be supported all their lives at the public expense; why they are to be put into a more fortunate case than clerks in mercantile and banking houses, and than many of our clergy, and of our military and naval officers.

On Financial Reform (London, 1830), pp.137-8, 207-11.

(c) RICHARD OASTLER

Oastler was one of the most persistent campaigners for legislative control of working conditions in factories. Once legislation had been passed, he pressed tirelessly for its proper enforcement. During the 1830s he published numerous pamphlets. The arguments in them are well represented in his evidence on 7 July 1832 to the Commons Select Committee on the labour of children in mills and factories.

9798. Where do you reside? — At Fixby Hall, near Huddersfield.
9799. Has your mind been latterly directed to the consideration

of the condition of the children and young persons engaged in the mills and factories of this country, with a view to affording them permanent legislative relief? — It has.

9800. What was your inducement for directing your mind to these considerations? — The immediate circumstance which led my attention to the facts, was a communication made to me by a very opulent spinner, that it was the regular custom, to work children in factories thirteen hours a day, and only allow them half an hour for dinner; that that was the regular custom, and that in many factories they were worked considerably more. I had previously observed a difference in the working classes of the West Riding of the county of York, I mean in the clothing districts. I had observed an amazing difference from what they are now, in comparison of what they were when I was a youth; but I must say that my attention had not been particularly called to the subject of the factory system, until I had that fact communicated to me, which certainly startled me considerably; and although it was communicated to me by an individual who must have been acquainted with the fact that it was true, I think I was three times pointedly addressing him, 'Is it really true? Is it really true?' Being assured that it was so, I resolved from that moment that I would dedicate every power of body and mind to this object, until these poor children were relieved from that excessive labour; and from that moment, which was the 29th of September 1830, I have never ceased to use every legal means, which I had it in my power to use, for the purpose of emancipating these innocent slaves. The very day on which the fact was communicated to me, I addressed a letter to the public, in the *Leeds Mercury*, upon the subject. I have since that had many opponents to contend against; but not one single fact which I have communicated has ever been contradicted or ever can be. I have certainly been charged by the opponents of the measure, in general germs, with exaggerations, but on all occasions I have refrained from exposing the worst parts of the system, for they are so gross that I dare not publish them. The demoralizing effects of the system are as bad, I know it, as the demoralizing effects of slavery in the West Indies. I know that there are instances and scenes of the grossest prostitution amongst the poor creatures who are the victims of the system, and in some cases are the objects of the cruelty and rapacity and sensuality of their masters. These things I never dared to publish, but the cruelties which are inflicted personally upon the little children, not to mention the immensely long hours which they are subject to work, are such as I am very sure would disgrace a West Indian plantation. On one occasion I was very singularly placed; I was in the company of a West India slave master and three Bradford spinners; they brought the two systems into fair comparison, and the spinners were obliged to be silent when the slave owner said, 'Well, I have always thought myself disgraced by being the owner of black slaves, but we never, in the West Indies, thought it was possible for any human being to be so cruel as to require a child of nine years old to work twelve hours and a half a day; and that, you acknowledge, is your regular practice.' I have seen little boys and girls of 10 years old; one I have in my eye particularly now, whose forehead has been cut open by the thong; whose cheeks and lips have been laid open, and whose back has been almost covered with black stripes; and the only crime that that little boy, who was 10 years and 3 months old, had committed, was that he retched three cardings, which are three pieces of woollen yarn, about three inches each long. The same boy told me that he had been frequently knocked down with the billy-roller, and that on one occasion, he had been hung up by a rope round the body, and almost frightened to death; but I am sure it is unnecessary for me to say any thing more upon the bodily sufferings that these poor creatures are subject to; I have seen their bodies almost broken down, so that they could not walk without assistance, when they have been 17 or 18 years of age. I know many cases of poor young creatures who have worked in factories, and who have been worn down by the system at the age of 16 and 17, and who, after living all their lives in this slavery, are kept in poor-houses, not by the masters for whom they have worked, as would be the case if they were negro slaves, but by other people who have reaped no advantage from their labour. These are the particular facts which I wish to state; and one which I would also call the attention of the Committee to, is the domestic system of manufacture which obtained in the West Riding of Yorkshire, when I was a boy; it was the custom for the children at that time, to mix learning their trades with other instruction and with amusement, and they learned their trades or their occupations, not by being put into places, to stop there from morning to night, but by having a little work to do, and then some little time for instruction, and they were generally under the immediate care of their parents; the villages about Leeds and Huddersfield were occupied by respectable little clothiers, who could manufacture a piece of cloth or two in the week, or three or four or five pieces, and always had their family at home; and they could at that time make a good profit by what they sold; there were filial affection and parental feeling, and not over-labour; but that race of manufacturers has been almost completely destroyed; there are scarcely any of the old-fashioned domestic manufacturers left, and the villages are composed of one or two, or in some cases of three or four, mill-owners, and the rest, poor creatures who are reduced and ground down to want, and in general are compelled to live upon the labour of their little ones; it is almost the general system for the little children in these manufacturing villages to know nothing of their parents at all excepting that in a morning very early, at 5 o'clock, very often before 4, they are awakened by a human being that they are told is their father, and are pulled out of bed (I have heard many a score of them give an account of it) when they are almost asleep, and lesser children are absolutely carried on the backs of the older children asleep to the mill, and they see no more of their parents, generally speaking, till they go home at night, and are sent to bed. Now that system must necessarily prevent the growth of filial affection. It destroys the happiness in the cottage family, and leads both parents and children not to regard each other in the way that Providence designed they should. It is a very common system, as soon as a child is enabled to earn a little more money than its board wages, for it to strike a bargain with its parent; when it gets to be 13 or 14 years old it will threaten to leave if they will not let it have so much of its wages; and they consider themselves quite free agents and under no control. With regard to the fathers, I have heard many of them declare that it is such a pain to them to think that they are kept by their little children, and that their little children are subjected to so many inconveniences that they scarcely know how to bear their lives; and I have heard many of them declare that they would much

rather be transported than be compelled to submit to it. I have heard mothers, more than on ten or eleven occasions, absolutely say that they would rather that their lives were ended than that they should live to be subjected to such misery. The general effect of the system is this, and they know it, to place a bonus upon crimes; because their little children, and their parents too, know that if they only commit theft and break the laws, they will be taken up and put into the House of Correction, and there they will not have to work more than six or seven hours a day. Such being the general state of things in the manufacturer's cottage, I think we need not be surprised at the present discontented, nay, one might almost say the disaffected state of the working classes. I think that arises from no other circumstance but that complete inversion of the law of nature, making the little children into slaves to work for their fathers and mothers, and leaving their fathers destitute in the streets to mourn over their sorrows; I believe that is the foundation of the disaffection and unpleasantness of the present age. The system is also manifestly unjust towards the proprietors of land, for when persons can get employment in these mills they are tempted to bring their families from agricultural districts and to dwell in the manufacturing villages; those that come are perhaps strong and healthy at first, but are completely ruined by the overworking which they are subjected to, and the moment they become useless they are sent back again to the agriculturists for support: these cases are very common indeed. This is a system which, in my opinion, ought to be reformed, if it were for nothing but this one consideration, that it gives in every little village, and every neighbourhood in the manufacturing districts, too much power into one man's hand. I mean to say that too large a proportion of the inhabitants of a district are invariably, by this system, subjected to the despotism of one individual, and that necessarily leads to what we call combinations, as the poor workman has no chance whatever of standing up for his own rights unless he combines with other workmen to support him.
9801. In your observations regarding the factory system, and the necessity of its regulation and revision, do you coincide with the views and feelings of those most deeply interested in the adjustment of this important question, namely, with the parties

that are the subjects of this system of cruelty and over-labour, which you have been describing? — I am quite sure that the operatives, if that is the party considered most interested, of the West Riding of the county of York, are decidedly of opinion that the Bill for regulating the labour in factories to ten hours a day, must pass. I am decidedly of opinion that they consider it as a thing which cannot be refused; and I am postively sure, if it is refused, that they will never cease to agitate the question until they obtain it.

Parliamentary Papers, HC 1831-32, xv (706), 454-6.

(d) EDWIN CHADWICK

The importance of Edwin Chadwick in the history of municipal, poor law and public health reform is well known. His work as an administrator and the achievement of his many reports are well documented. It is useful to cite here an example of his methods as a lobbyist. During the battle over the second reading of the Poor Law Amendment Bill, Chadwick decided to go to the House of Commons and hand direct to Members a tract on centralization. Already firmly opposed to the ideas behind the Bill, 'The Times' launched a violent attack on such behaviour.

We had not intended to waste another word upon the senseless trash contained in a pamphlet which is entitled *The Principles of Delegated, Central and Special Authority, applied to the Poor Laws' Amendment Bill*. We return to it, however, upon learning that its author, or his admirers (probably both), beset the House of Commons on Friday evening, and thrust a copy of the rubbish into the hands of every hon. member as he entered or quitted the house. We thought at the first perusal of the pamphlet that we could hit upon the quarter from which it emanated; and this piece of impertinence on the part of the author, or his friends, or both, convinces us that our conjecture was right. If any one of any set of men but a member of the *Westminster Rump* could have made so low an estimate of the intellects of the members of the House of Commons as this spoil-paper pamphleteer made, when he supposed he could palm such nonsense upon them as matter worth a moment's consideration, still it would hardly have been possible to find a man rude and insolent enough to take this pointed mode of *telling* the members of the House of

Commons to their very teeth, how gullible he thought them, unless the individual were looked for among the *Rump* of Westminster, who had the brazen effrontery to import from a neighbouring country, and to publish it here, a plan as disgusting as it was demoralizing for removing all the fears of MR MALTHUS as to surplus population. In this workshop, we have no doubt, these 'principles' have been forged; but whether they be the handywork of some sucking SOLON of the Benthamite breed, or whether they have employed the leisure of some retired and superannuated sage of the same spawn, we will not pretend to determine, because the imbecility of old age is not always distinguishable from the feebleness of youth, and because conceit being the staple commodity of this republican firm, which have all things in common, the youngest usually pounces upon as large a share of it as the oldest . . . For the present we content outselves with cautioning our readers, that there is one very serious point of view in which we should consider the advocacy of the creation of novel and arbitrary powers, when that advocacy proceeds from professed republicans, as the advocacy of the arbitrary and irresponsible tribunal, to be called the *Central Board*, has proceeded from professed republicans, whether the writer of this pamphlet be one of them or whether he be not . . . If such a measure, which is a step towards doing without both KING and Parliament, be not as great a dimming of the lustre of Royalty, and as destructive a cramping and crippling of the powers of Parliament, as any that the most *farouche republicain* could have desired or devised — why then the schemes and the expectations of this low faction must be as inordinate and boundless as is the folly of those who are unconsciously playing their game for them. No wonder the republicans throw up their greasy hats, and cry *huzza* for the Poor Laws' Amendment Bill!

The Times, 20 May 1834.

18 Contemporary Attitudes to the Functions of Government

(a) SIR HENRY TAYLOR

Taylor was writing from his experience in the Colonial Office.

Concerning the Constitution of an office or establishment for transacting the business of a minister.

In this country an establishment of this kind is commonly formed as follows:- 1st. There are one or more political and parliamentary officers subordinate to the minister, who come and go with their principals or with the government to which they belong, but have not seats in the cabinet. They go by the name of Under Secretaries of State in the three Secretaries of State's offices, Vice-President of the Board of Trade, Secretaries and junior Lords or junior Commissioners at the Board of Treasury, the Board of Admiralty, and the Board of Control. 2nd. There is an officer of similar rank, who is not in parliament and holds his office by a more permanent tenure, without reference to changes of ministry. 3rd. There is the minister's private secretary, who of course comes and goes with his principal, whether the change extends to the government or not. 4th. There are some twenty clerks more or less, also permanent, divided into three or four grades of subordination.

As any essential reform of the executive government must consist in a reform of these establishments, I will endeavour to explain what seems to be the theory of them, what are their merits in practice, and what are the means of amending them.

The system seems to assume that a minister who is charged with a particular branch of business besides his share in the general direction of affairs in the cabinet, will require for that branch of business, one person or more to assist him in transactions of a political and parliamentary character, and another to aid him with that knowledge and experience connected with his particular charge which can only be obtained by continuous service in one department of state; and that he will also require a private secretary to write his complimentary notes and take care of his confidential papers, and a score of clerks to transact matters of routine and make copies and entries of despatches. — The theory is correct in assuming that these several things are necessary to be done; but it is exceedingly fallacious in its estimate of relative quantities, and in its omissions.

A statesman who takes a part in consultations in the cabinet, or debates in a legislative assembly, or in both, ought to be relieved from all business which is not accessory to the performance of his duties as councillor and legislator. For these duties, if amply and energetically performed, must, by their nature if not by their magnitude, incapacitate any but very extraordinary individuals for performing others. The excitement of oral discussion with able colleagues upon deeply interesting and often personal topics, and still more the excitement of public debate, can rarely be combined with patient application to dry documentary business within the walls of an office . . . It is true that no accurate demarcation can be made between parliamentary and cabinet business on the one hand, and office business on the other; and a good deal of acquaintance with the latter will be necessary to give the general knowledge required for the former . . . the statesman who is dependent for his place upon a majority in the House of Commons, must be responsible for everything; and in order to bear this responsibility he must be conversant with all the more important business transacted under his authority. This conversancy I would be understood, therefore, to include in the business accessory to the discharge of a minister's duties in the cabinet and in parliament; the exemption which I require for him being of that actual execution of his office business which is not indispensable to a competent degree of conversancy with it.

The minister being thus relieved during the whole year, and his parliamentary assistant during the session of parliament, it remains to inquire how the office business (setting aside the mere routine and mechanical part) is to be done without their help . . .

In all cases concerning points of conduct and quarrels of subordinate officers, in all cases of individual claims upon individuals, in short in all cases (and such commonly constitute the bulk of a minister's unpolitical business) wherein the minister is called upon to deliver a quasi-judicial decision, he should on no consideration permit himself to pronounce such decision unaccompanied by a detailed statement of all the material facts and reasons upon which his judgment proceeds . . .

Further, it is one business to do what must be done, another to devise what ought to be done. It is in the spirit of the British government, as hitherto existing, to transact only the former business; and the reform which it requires is to enlarge that spirit so as to include the latter. Of and from amongst those measures which are forced upon him, to choose that which will bring him the most credit with the least trouble, has hitherto been the sole care of a statesman in office; and as a statesman's official establishment has been heretofore constituted, it is care enough for any man. Every day, every hour, has its exigencies, its immediate demands; and he who has hardly time to eat his meals, cannot be expected to occupy himself in devising good for mankind . . . The current compulsory business he gets through as he may; some is undone, some is ill done; but at least to get it done is an object which he proposes to himself. But as to the inventive and suggestive portions of a statesman's func-tions, he would think himself an Utopian dreamer if he undertook them in any other way than through a re-constitution and reform of his establishment . . .

This then is the great evil and want — that there is not within the pale of our government any adequately numerous body of efficient statesmen, some to be more externally active and answer the demands of the day, others to be somewhat more retired and meditative in order that they may take thought for the morrow . . .

It is in the first place indispensable to a reform of the executive government of this country, that every minister of state charged with a particular department of public business should be provided with four or six permanent under-secretaries instead of one, — that all of those four or six should be efficient closet-statesmen, and two of them at the least be endowed, in addition to their practical abilities, with some gifts of philosophy and speculation well cultivated, disciplined, and prepared for use . . . I hardly know if that minister has existed in the present generation, who, if such a mind were casually presented to him, would not forego the use of it rather than hazard a debate in the House of Commons upon an additional item in his estimates.

Till the government of the country shall become a nucleus at which the best wisdom in the country contained shall be perpetually forming itself in deposit, it will be, except as regards the shuffling of power from hand to hand and class to class, little better than a government of fetches, shifts, and hand-to-mouth expedients. Till a wise and constant instrumentality at work upon administrative measures (distinguished as they might be from measures of political parties) shall be understood to be essential to the government of a country, that country can be considered to enjoy nothing more than the embryo of a government, — a means towards producing, through changes in its own structure and constitution and in the political elements acting upon it, something worthy to be called a government at some future time . . .

Henry Taylor, *The Statesman* (London, 1836), pp.146-64.

(b) JOHN WADE

The 'Extraordinary Black Book' came out originally in 1820 in serial form. Many further editions were published as complete books with numerous additions. It may be described as a catalogue of every sinecure position available in the United Kingdom and included 'lists of Pluralists, Placemen, Pensioners and Sinecurists . . . ' and presented 'a complete view of the expenditure, patronage, influence and abuses of the government, in Church, State, Law and Representation'. Wade was himself granted a civil list pension in 1862.

A Statement of the Annual Expenditure of the United Kingdom, in Salaries, Pensions, Sinecures, Half-pay, Superannuations, Compensations and Allowances.

Salaries of 22,912 persons employed in the public offices	£2,788,907
Retired full-pay, half-pay, superannuations, pensions and allowances in the army	2,939,652

Retired full-pay, half-pay, superannuations, pensions and allowances in the Navy	1,583,797
Retired full-pay, half-pay, superannuations, pensions and allowances in the Ordnance	374,987
Superannuated allowances in the civil departments of government	478,967
Pensions	777,556
Pensions in the nature of compensations for the loss of offices in England	12,020
Pensions in the nature of compensations for the loss of offices in Ireland, chiefly in consequence of the Union	89,245
Annual value of sinecure offices	356,555
Commissioners of Inquiry	56,299
	£9,457,985

Can any one believe that, in these few items, a saving of at least three millions might not be effected? And with a saving even to this amount, how many oppressive taxes might be repealed! If we further extend our view to other departments of the government, and to the courts of law, the civil list, the colonies, the monopolies of the Bank and East India Company, the established church, and the corn-laws, what an ample field presents itself to our consideration for the relief of this suffering and oppressed community.

But will government ever avail itself of these vast resources as the means of national amelioration? Never: it is impossible under the existing system. Effective retrenchment, without a previous parliamentary reform, is a chimera. To retrench is to *weaken*; the true policy of the Oligarchy is to spend, not to save. There are, no doubt, scores, nay, hundreds of offices and establishments useless, indeed, to the people, but invaluable to their rulers. The greater the sinecure, the greater its importance to the Aristocracy; and the very reason urged by the people for its extinction, is the strongest argument for its retention by their oppressors. Could government only reward its servants according to their deserts, what inducement would there be to enter into its service? Who would incur the odium of such employment! How could it obtain adherents? How could it so long have had zealous supporters in every part of the empire, and carried on a detestable system, subversive of the

117

rights, and incompatible with the happiness of the community?

Ever since the death of Fox and Pitt there has been scarcely an individual with the least pretension to the endowments of a statesman in the administration. Look over the roll of the Percevals, Vansittarts, Castlereaghs, Jenkinsons, Cannings, Sidmouths, Huskissons, and Scotts, and say, if there is one that did not deserve a halter, or whose proper place was not behind a counter, in lieu of directing the resolves of a legislative assembly. Yet by these, and such as these, were the destinies of this great empire swayed for upwards of twenty years. Can we wonder at the frightful results of their empyrical statesmanship? Can we wonder that they bequeathed to their successors, convulsion, decay and death, in every fibre of the kingdom? But incapable, vile and unprincipled as these men were, ignorant and reckless, as experience has proved them to be, of the ultimate issues of their measures; still these scions of the Pitt school were too sagacious ever to think that retrenchment and rotten boroughs were compatible elements of the constitution. They knew better; they had been too long familiar with the secret pulses and springs of the state machinery to commit so egregious a mistake. Their dependence was on *force* and *corruption*; on the bayonets of the military, and the annual expenditure of eighty millions of money. These formed the right and left hands, the master principles of their policy. The support they could not bribe they sought to intimidate. Such was their black and iron system; it lasted *their time*, or the time of most of the pillaging and hypocritical crew; and for anything beyond they did not care a rush!

Let us hope that we are on the eve of better times, that we shall not be deluded by temporary expedients and professions, put forth merely to gain time for plundering, nor quack remedies to be followed by mortal maladies; in short, let us hope the new ministry will proceed on scientific principles, and that we shall have a parliamentary reform first, and next such an effective retrenchment and disposition of public burthens as well afford real national relief.

'Corruption wins not more than honesty'; and the true end of government is not difficult to attain. It is simply to augment social happiness — affording equal security to the property and persons of every individual, — protecting the weak against the strong, — the poor against the rich; in short, by guarding against the extremes of indigence and crime, luxury and vice, and spreading an equilibrium of comfort and enjoyment through all ranks, by good laws, wisely conceived, promptly and impartially administered.

It is a cheap and admirable contrivance, when established on the rights, and supported by the confidence of the public. There is then no need of standing armies in time of peace. There is no need of expending sixteen millions a year in support of naval and military establishments. There is no need of a Sinking Fund as a resource for future war. Government is strong in the affections of the people. It is prepared for every exigence, and must always be invincible against domestic foes and foreign aggressors. But, if government has not this support; if it is looked upon only as an instrument of rapacity and extortion; if it is looked upon as a legalized system of pillage, fraud and delusion; if it is looked upon only as an artful cabal of tyrants united for plunder and oppression; then must such a government, instead of being a cheap and simple institution, be a complex and expensive establishment — strong, not in the people, but in its means of corruption, delusion and intimidation.

The English government has been long approximating to the latter predicament. It has ceased to possess the respect and confidence of the people, and has governed by over-awing the weak, deluding the ignorant, and corrupting the baser part of the community. The latter — its power of corruption — its means of rewarding its adherents by the *spoil of the people*, is the great lever by which it has operated.

Black Book (London, 1831), pp.412-4.

(c) ANTHONY TROLLOPE

Trollope was employed in the General Post Office from 1834 to 1841 and from 1841 to 1866 as a travelling surveyor of the posts.

Sir Francis Freeling was followed at the Post Office by Colonel Maberly, who certainly was not my friend. I do not know that I deserved to find a friend in my new master, but I think that a man with better judgment would not have formed so low an opinion of me as he did. Years have gone by, and I can write now, and almost feel, without anger; but I can remember well the keenness of my anguish when I was treated as though I were unfit for any useful work. I did struggle — not to do the work, for there was nothing which was not easy without any struggling — but to show that I was willing to do it. My bad character nevertheless stuck to me, and was not to be got rid of by any efforts within my power. I do admit that I was irregular. It was not considered to be much in my favour that I could write letters — which was mainly the work of our office — rapidly, correctly, and to the purpose. The man who came at ten, and who was always still at his desk at half-past four, was preferred before me, though when at his desk he might be less efficient. Such preference was no doubt proper; but, with a little encouragement, I also would have been punctual. I got credit for nothing and was reckless.

As it was, the conduct of some of us was very bad. There was a comfortable sitting-room upstairs, devoted to the use of some one of our number who in turn was required to remain on the place all night. Hither one or two of us would adjourn after lunch, and play *écarté* for an hour or two. I do not know whether such ways are possible now in our public offices. And here we used to have suppers and card-parties at night — great symposiums, with much smoking of tobacco; for in one part of the building there lived a whole bevy of clerks. These were gentlemen whose duty it then was to make up and receive the foreign mails. I do not remember that they worked later or earlier than the other sorting-clerks; but there was supposed to be something special in foreign letters, which required that the men who handled them should have minds undistracted by the outer world. Their salaries, too, were higher than those of their more homely brethren; and they paid nothing for their lodgings. Consequently there was a somewhat fast set in those apartments, given to cards and to tobacco, who drank spirits and water in preference to tea. I was not one of them, but was a good deal with them.

Anthony Trollope, *An Autobiography* (1883, cited from reprint edn, Fontana, 1962), pp.52-3.

19 Reform within the Departments:
Sir James Graham at the Admiralty

The achievements of Graham were considerable both in terms of economy and efficiency. He was the first minister to show signs of understanding the need for proper accounting procedures in government departments if parliamentary control of spending was to mean anything at all. He also realised that departmental business must be reorganised and talent recruited into departments if the work was to be adequately done.

(a) ACCOUNTING

I have always been struck by the evidence which came across me of the great work which Sir James Graham did at the Admiralty in the Grey Ministry of 1830.

From a financial point of view, he was the first statesman who grasped the method in which alone the financial control over the expenditure can be secured.

Up to his time the House of Commons had no control whatever. They voted estimates, but they had no information as to how the money they granted was actually spent, except an *ipse dixit* of the spending Department. The financial authorities of the House, in and out of office, bewildered themselves in attempts to control expenditure before it actually took place. Sir James Graham saw, and *saw first*, that the only real check on expenditure is to be found in a Report to the House of Commons on that expenditure, when it has taken place, by an independent auditor; and he passed an Act requiring such an account of Naval expenditure to be prepared *for the House of Commons* by the Commissioners of Audit, and presented yearly.

That Report has been presented yearly since 1832, and it has been the precedent extended gradually to the whole of the public expenditure. He did not see that his check would not be really effected unless provision was also made for the House of Commons examining that account. This defect was remedied by Mr Gladstone much later, in 1860, when he established the Standing Committee of the House of Commons on Public Accounts. That Committee examines the Auditor's Report on

121

the Naval expenditure item by item, and reports to the House its conclusions.

Sir James Graham, however, may lay claim to being the first statesman to understand and enforce the only real check on public expenditure; and that achievement establishes him with financial students as a great financial authority, and a great administrator.

Letter from Lord Welby, 27 September 1905, in C.S. Parker, *Sir James Graham*, (London, 1907), i, 165-6.

(b) OFFICE PROCEDURES

The two naval administrations of Sir James Graham will long be remembered — the first as the one which reorganised the Navy, and effected all the important changes so much needed in the civil departments, such as the abolition of the Navy Board, Victualling Board, etc., and the second for the zeal and ability displayed in the preparation of the fleets upon the outbreak of the Crimean war, and the brilliant success which characterised the management of the transport service, in the conveyance of troops and stores.

One of the first measures adopted by the new Board was to reverse at once the naval policy of their predecessors, who had persisted for years in spending hundreds of thousands annually upon vessels inadequate in size and deficient in armament to compete successfully with the new classes of vessels in course of construction in the dockyards of France and of the United States . . .

So fully impressed was Sir James Graham with the urgent necessity of establishing a permanent school for the scientific and practical teaching of gunnery to the naval officers and seamen of the fleet, that he decided to commission at once a ship for that purpose.

To him and his Board is due the credit of taking the initiative in reducing the number of officers upon the active list, and adopting many salutary measures calculated to ensure the employment of deserving officers.

But the reform to which perhaps the country will attach the greatest importance was the abolition of the Navy Office and

Victualling Board, and the placing of the civil departments of the Navy under the individual responsibility of five principal officers, each to be superintended by a member of the Board of Admiralty. This division of duty was established on so sound a basis that after sixty years it still remains in full force. The system has proved not only to be sound in theory, but to have worked successfully when put to the test of practical experience . . .

By this arrangement the whole business of the Admiralty was brought under the eye of the First Lord, as well as the cognisance of every member of the Board, each individual being thus afforded an opportunity of giving expression to his opinions.

So convinced was Sir James Graham of the great advantages of inter-communication between the principal Officers of State, that he habitually discussed the nature of the communications he proposed to write with the Minister of the Department before making the written communication, and thereby much needless correspondence and misunderstanding was judiciously avoided . . .

Sir James Graham was never seen to greater advantage than at the head of the Board-room table. He was peculiarly happy in extracting from the several members of the Board the particular information he was desirous of eliciting, and then placing all the facts before them in so plain, clear, and simple a manner as to carry their opinions with him.

It is no easy matter for a First Lord to keep the attention of the various members directed to the particular subject under discussion. This can only be accomplished by occasionally putting questions to them, which if they were not paying due attention it would be impossible for them to answer. Sir James did this with such adroitness as to excite the admiration of those who were silent listeners, and could plainly perceive the force and spirit of the interrogations, when attention and interest were beginning to wane. He instantly put a stop to all irrelevant discussions . . .

Sir James detailed to the Secretary the wording of every minute and in most important cases himself drew up the answer. This he did with rapidity and clearness of expression, upon a sheet of notepaper, which would cover, when copied, several pages of foolscap. The amount of work he would transact in the course of a morning was perfectly wonderful!

Sir James Graham possessed such personal influence in the Cabinet of Earl Grey, and generally laid his case before the Ministry with such power and cogency of argument, that he rarely failed in bringing conviction to their minds, and carrying his point to a successful issue.

The views of Sir John Briggs, *ibid*, i, 152-4.

IV

Greater Pressures:
the 1850s

The early 1850s saw a change in the focus of attention for administrative reformers inside and outside Parliament. The argument for economy more noticeably gave way to that for efficiency. The inherent contradictions in these arguments were only rarely voiced. Administrative inefficiencies and inadequacies revealed in the conduct of the Crimean War provided strong weapons for the reformers.

20 Problems of
Parliamentary Procedure

THOMAS ERSKINE MAY

Although the House of Commons had been enabled by its procedural forms to achieve more sophisticated legislative functions in the 1830s and 1840s, the cards in the game between the executive and the private members for parliamentary time remained stacked very much in favour of the latter. May, later Clerk of the house, described the problem.

The last twenty years have been a period of the most extraordinary legislative activity that has ever been known in any country, in the enjoyment of settled laws and institutions. It may be sufficient to remind the reader, that amidst an enormous amount of general and miscellaneous legislation (of which the Statute Book alone can be a sufficient record), the representative system in England, Scotland, and Ireland, has been entirely reconstructed — the Municipal Corporations of those countries have been reconstituted — the civil disabilities of the Roman Catholics and other religious bodies have been removed — the Church Establishment in England and Ireland has been revised — our Criminal Code has been twice reviewed and amended — increased facilities have been provided for the civil administration of justice — the Poor laws of England have been remodelled — a legal provision for the poor introduced for the first time into Ireland — and a general system of Poor Relief provided for Scotland. Slavery has been abolished in all our colonies — the ancient Charter of the East India Company has been re-considered, and freedom of commerce extended to the East — the Charter of the Bank of England has been twice revised in connexion with our monetary laws — the entire system of banking in England, Scotland, and Ireland, has been regulated — and (not further to multiply examples), our commercial, financial, and fiscal policy has undergone the most extensive and fundamental alterations.

In a period of twenty years, from 1828 to 1847, inclusive, 2040 public, and 4056 local and personal and private Acts have been enacted by Parliament: and many of the public Acts, having consolidated all previous laws upon the same subject, are codes of laws in themselves, rather than ordinary statutes.

Nothing but ignorance or oblivion of these facts can favour an opinion that Parliament has been inactive, or that its laborious deliberations have been unfruitful of results. Laws of extraordinary importance have been successfully enacted, and have, for the most part, received the general approbation of the country. The great objects of the legislature have been attained — but with what labour — with what straining and difficulty — with what waste of time, energy and health — with what vexations and disappointments to Ministers and Members of both Houses, none can have an adequate conception but those who have closely watched the harrassing business of practical legislation . . .

Having suggested various remedies for the delays regularly experienced in general debate and at various stages of bill procedure, May turned to the problem of adjourned debates.

This evil would undoubtedly be mitigated by restrictions upon the length of debates, but still more, by a careful distribution of the public business. Important Government measures ought never to be permitted to clash with one another. They must, of course be advanced or suspended according to their relative political exigencies; but it rarely happens that two or more considerable measures can be successfully advanced at the same time. The rule should be to proceed, so far as circumstances will permit, with one measure at a time, until it has advanced so far, that its progress may be suspended for a season, without inconvenience. But in every arrangement of this kind, the Government find themselves surrounded with difficulties, as they have no means of ensuring the continuance of a debate from day to day, and all their calculations are disturbed by frequent adjournments. So much is always expected from the Government, that they may reasonably claim further facilities for carrying on the public business. The proposed addition of Thursday to the Government nights, at an early period of the Session, as well as the alterations in practice which have been suggested, would facilitate the progress of Government measures; but it is also essential that, in certain cases, the adjourned debate upon an important question should take precedence of all other business, until it is completed, and arrangements should be made by which the other business should be subjected to as little disturbance as possible. For example, if a debate continued for a week, all the Notices of Motions and Orders of the Day, standing in the Order-book for that week, might be transferred, in the same order, to the ensuing week, and take precedence of the other business already set down for each day. If a debate should be adjourned upon a Motion, made upon a Notice night, it should take precedence of all notices on the ensuing notice day . . .

He concluded that his ideas:

Have been framed in furtherance of the spirit and intention of the ancient rules of the House, and with the sole object of forwarding the dispatch of business, consistently with the due consideration of every public measure, and with the utmost freedom of debate.

Erskine May, *Remarks and Suggestions with a View to Facilitate the Dispatch of Public Business in Parliament* (London, 1849), pp. 4-6, 35-6.

21 Salaries in the Public
Offices in 1850

SELECT COMMITTEE REPORT

This Select Committee focused particularly on the size and cost of the establishments of the chief government departments. Members were particularly interested in the relationship of the Treasury with other departments and called first as a witness Sir Charles Wood, the Chancellor of the Exchequer.

32. Chairman. Have the duties of your office increased or diminished since the last period when they came under the revision of Parliament? — They have increased very considerably.

33. Will you state in what way they have increased? — They have increased in consequence of the much larger amount of business which has been in various ways thrown upon the different offices, including the Treasury, and also from the increased duty, which is very properly placed more and more every year upon the Treasury, of exercising a more rigorous control over the expenditure of all other departments, which brings to us a much greater amount of work than was formerly performed by the Treasury.

34. Has that increased amount of work been of the same nature as that which was performed before, or have any additional departments been thrown upon the Chancellor of the Exchequer? — I speak of the Chancellor of the Exchequer as acting as the head of the Treasury. The increased amount of work thrown upon the Treasury is principally of the same character as before that of controlling expenditure. In almost every department of the Government there has been a great increase of business. So far as that increase of business involves the expenditure of money, reference must be had to the Treasury; for example, the Treasury has to regulate the salaries of the Inspectors under the Home Office, and the travelling and other expenses of all persons employed. All questions in money matters connected with the colonies come under the Treasury;

every sort of expense, whether in the civil Government at home or in the civil Government abroad, comes necessarily under the Treasury. The number of references to us, both in registered papers and in unofficial communications, has very much increased with the general increase of business thrown upon the Government . . .

40. Mr *Ricardo*. The financial affairs of every department are not under the control of the Chancellor of the Exchequer entirely, are they; for instance, to what extent is the Admiralty under your control? — The Estimates of all the departments are submitted for the sanction of the Treasury, and no expenditure can be incurred, beyond that which is sanctioned by the Treasury.

Having surveyed the salaries paid and the jobs done in the different departments, the Committee recommended little change.

. . . Your Committee first selected those Offices which from the nature of the duties attached to them, have always been considered of the greatest importance in a Government; namely, those of First Lord of the Treasury, the Chancellor of the Exchequer, the Three Secretaries of State, and the First Lord of the Admiralty. For these Offices it is requisite to secure the services of men who combine the highest talents with the greatest experience in public affairs; and considering the rank and importance of the Offices, and the labours and responsibilities incurred by those who hold them. Your Committee are of opinion, that the salaries of these Offices were settled in 1831 at the lowest amount which is consistent with the requirements of the Public Service.

Select Committee Report on Official Salaries, *Parliamentary Papers*, HC 1850 xv (611), pp. v, 5.

22 The Setting Up of the Northcote-Trevelyan Inquiry, 1853

The activities of the Financial Reform movement and a series of revelations of frauds and abuses in some government departments in the late 1840s and 1850s encouraged Gladstone to inaugurate a general inquiry into the organization of the civil service. For the purpose he chose Sir Charles Trevelyan, who, after fourteen years in the Indian civil service, had entered the Treasury as Assistant Secretary in 1840, and proved the dominant partner in the exercise, and Sir Stafford Northcote, previously Gladstone's secretary.

The Chancellor of the Exchequer states . . . that his attention has been called to the inquiries which are in progress under the superintendence of the Treasury into the establishment of various public departments, for the purpose of considering applications for increase of salary, abolishing or consolidating redundant offices, supplying additional assistance where it is required, getting rid of obsolete processes, and introducing more simple and compendious modes of transacting business, establishing a proper distinction between intellectual and mechanical labour, and, generally, so revising and readjusting the public establishments as to place them on the footing best calculated for the efficient discharge of their important functions, according to the actual circumstances of the present time.

In connexion with these inquiries into each particular establishment, it is highly necessary that the conditions which are common to all the public offices, such as the preliminary testimonials of character and bodily health to be required from candidates for public employment, the examination into their intellectual attainments, and the regulation of the promotions, should be carefully considered, so as to attain every practicable security for the public that none but qualified persons will be appointed, and that they will afterwards have every practicable inducement to the active discharge of their duties.

The general result of these inquiries and of the proceedings which will be taken upon them, will, undoubtedly, be that the public service will be conducted in a more efficient manner by a smaller number of persons than is the case at present. The gain in point of economy will probably be important. Five thousand pounds a year was saved by the recent revision of the Chief Secretary's Office, and the offices connected with it in London and in Dublin; and the ultimate reduction of expenditure in consequence of the arrangements in progress at the Board of Trade will amount to upwards of five thousand pounds. But the gain in point of efficiency will be far greater. The object is, that the business of the public should be done in the best and most economical manner; and that arrangement of the public establishments which most conduces to this result will, in almost every case, be the most economical.

Their Lordships' Assistant Secretary has of late years taken an active part in the Committees of Inquiry which have been appointed for this object, and it is desirable that the experience which he has acquired both as a member of these Committees and in the ordinary discharge of his duty at the Treasury, which is the central office for the revision of the public establishments, should be turned to the best account.

The Chancellor of the Exchequer proposed that Sir Stafford Northcote, who acquired an extensive acquaintance with the public departments during his employment at the Board of Trade, and has proved on many occasions his superior fitness for administrative functions, should be joined with Sir Charles Trevelyan in this important duty, and that he should give up his whole time to it. Sir Stafford Northcote has been actively employed for some weeks, under their Lordships' appointment, as a member of the Committee for inquiring into the establishments of the Privy Council Office and the Board of Trade, and the departments of Practical Art and Science, and the other offices dependent upon the Board of Trade.

My Lords entirely concur in the view which has been taken of this subject by the Chancellor of the Exchequer, and they are pleased to determine that Sir Stafford Northcote shall be paid at the rate of one thousand pounds a year for this service from the date of his first employment upon it, which salary will be paid from Civil Contingencies until further arrangements are made.

Direct the Paymaster-General to pay to Sir Stafford Northcote, in remuneration of his services as member of committees for inquiring into various public establishments with a view to a more efficient and economical performance of the public business, a salary of one thousand pounds a year until further orders, commencing on the 15th February last inclusively, and to charge the payments made by him under this direction to the account of Civil Contingencies.

Treasury Minute, 12 April 1853, *Parliamentary Papers*, HC 1854-55, xxx (439), 1-2.

23 The Northcote-Trevelyan Report

In November 1853 Northcote and Trevelyan presented their Report. It was brief, only twenty pages, but was to prove of fundamental importance in the development of the British civil service from a sort of clerkly employment into a profession capable of attracting men of ability and education. It was met by an immediate outcry from those sections of society which benefited extensively from the current patronage arrangements, and sustained resistance from both inside and outside government departments was maintained. Many of the suggestions in the report had already been tried in some departments as has already been seen in the case of the Admiralty (pp.121-4). Recruitment by open competitive examination had already been agreed in principle for the Indian civil service, but was yet to be tried. Full implementation of the recommendations for the home civil service was not achieved for twenty years and then met a number of obstacles in the departments of state.

. . . That the Permanent Civil Service, with all its defects, essentially contributes to the proper discharge of the functions of Government, has been repeatedly admitted by those who have successively been responsible for the conduct of our affairs. All, however, who have had occasion to examine its constitution with care, have felt that its organization is far from perfect, and that its amendment is deserving of the most careful attention . . . Admission into the Civil Service is indeed eagerly sought after, but it is for the unambitious, and the indolent or incapable, that it is chiefly desired. Those whose abilities do not warrant an expectation that they will succeed in the open professions, where they must encounter the competition of their contemporaries, and those whom indolence of temperament or physical infirmities unfit for active exertions, are placed in the Civil Service, where they may obtain an honourable livelihood with little labour, and with no risk; where their success depends upon their simply avoiding any flagrant misconduct, and attending with moderate regularity to routine duties; and in which they are secured against the ordinary consequences of old age, or failing health, by an arrangement which provides them with the means of supporting themselves after they have become incapacitated.

It may be noticed in particular that the comparative lightness of the work, and the certainty of provision in case of retirement owing to bodily incapacity, furnish strong inducements to the parents and friends of sickly youths to endeavour to obtain for them employment in the service of the Government . . . there are probably very few who have chosen this line of life with a view to raising themselves to public eminence . . .

There are, however, numerous honourable exceptions to these observations, and the trustworthiness of the entire body is unimpeached. They are much better than we have any right to expect from the system under which they are appointed and promoted.

The peculiar difficulties under which the Permanent Civil Service labours, in obtaining a good supply of men, as compared with other professions, are partly natural and partly artificial.

Its natural difficulties are such as these:

Those who enter it generally do so at an early age, when there has been no opportunity of trying their fitness for business, or forming a trustworthy estimate of their characters and abilities. This to a great extent is the case in other professions also, but those professions supply a corrective which is wanting in the Civil Service, for as a man's success in them depends upon his obtaining and retaining the confidence of the public, and as he is exposed to a sharp competition on the part of his contemporaries, those only can maintain a fair position who possess the requisite amount of ability and industry for the proper discharge of their duties. The able and energetic rise to the top; the dull and inefficient remain at the bottom. In the public establishments, on the contrary, the general rule is that all rise together. After a young man has been once appointed, the public have him for life; and if he is idle or inefficient, provided he does not grossly misconduct himself, we must either submit to have a portion of the public business inefficiently and discreditably performed, or must place the incompetent person on the retired list, with a pension, for the rest of his life. The feeling of security which this state of things necessarily engenders tends to encourage indolence, and thereby to depress the character of the Service. Again, those who are admitted into it at an early age are thereby relieved from the necessity of those struggles which for the most part fall to the lot of such as enter upon the open professions; their course is one of quiet, and generally of secluded, performance of routine duties, and they consequently have but limited opportunities of acquiring that varied experience of life which is so important to the development of character.

To these natural difficulties may be added others arising from what may be called artificial causes.

The character of the young men admitted to the public service depends chiefly upon the discretion with which the heads of departments, and others who are entrusted with the distribution of patronage, exercise that privilege. In those cases in which the patronage of departments belongs to their chief for the time being, the appointments which it commonly falls to his lot to make are either those of junior clerks, to whom no very important duties are in the first instance to be assigned, or of persons who are to fill responsible and highly paid situations above the rank of the ordinary clerkships. In the first case, as the character and abilities of the new junior clerk will produce but little immediate effect upon the office, the chief of the department is naturally led to regard the selection as a matter of small moment, and will probably bestow the office upon the son or dependant of some one having personal or political claims upon him, or perhaps upon the son of some meritorious public servant, without instituting any very minute inquiry into the merits of the young man himself. It is true that in many offices some kind of examination is prescribed, and that in almost all the person appointed is in the first instance nominated on probation; but, as will presently be pointed out, neither of these tests are at present very efficacious. The young man thus admitted is commonly employed upon duties of the merest routine. Many of the first years of his service are spent in copying papers, and other work of an almost mechanical character. In two or three years he is as good as he can be at such an employment. The remainder of his official life can only exercise a depressing influence on him, and renders the work of the office distasteful to him. Unlike the pupil in a conveyancer's or special pleader's office, he not only begins with mechanical labour as an introduction to labour of a higher kind, but often also ends with it. In the meantime his salary is gradually advancing till he reaches, by seniority, the top of his class, and on the occurrence of a vacancy in the class above him he is promoted to fill it, as a matter of course, and without any regard to his previous services or his qualifications. Thus, while no pains have been taken in the first instance to secure a good man for the office, nothing has been done after the clerk's appointment to turn his abilities, whatever they may be, to the best account. The result naturally is, that when the chief of the office has to make an appointment of visible and immediate importance to the efficiency of his department, he sometimes has difficulty in finding a clerk capable of filling it, and he is not unfrequently obliged to go out of the office, and to appoint some one of high standing in an open profession, or some one distinguished in other walks of life, over the heads of men who have been for many years in the public service. This is necessarily discouraging to the Civil Servants, and tends to strengthen in them the injurious conviction, that their success does not depend upon their own exertions, and that if they work hard, it will not advance them, — if they waste their time in idleness, it will not keep them back . . .

One more peculiarity in the Civil Service remains to be noticed. It is what may be called its fragmentary character . . . Each man's experience, interests, hopes, and fears are limited to the special branch of service in which he is himself engaged. The effect naturally is, to cramp the energies of the whole body, to encourage the growth of narrow views and departmental prejudices, to limit the acquisition of experience, and to repress and almost extinguish the spirit of emulation and competition; besides which, considerable inconvenience results from the want of facilities for transferring strength from an office where the work is becoming slack to one in which it is increasing, and from the consequent necessity of sometimes keeping up particular departments on a scale beyond their actual requirements . . .

What is the best method of providing it [the public service] with a supply of good men, and of making the most of them after they have been admitted? . . . Our opinion is, that, as a general rule, it is decidedly best to train young men . . . The maintenance of discipline is also easier under such circumstances, and regular habits may be enforced, which it would be difficult to impose for the first time upon older men. To these advantages must be added the important one of being able, by proper regulations, to secure the services of fit persons on much more economical terms . . .

The general principle, then, which we advocate is, that the public service should be carried on by the admission into its lower ranks of a carefully selected body of young men, who should be employed from the first upon work suited to their capacities and their education, and should be made constantly to feel that their promotion and future prospects depend entirely on the industry and ability with which they discharge their duties, that with average abilities and reasonable application they may look forward confidently to a certain provision for their lives, that with superior powers they may rationally hope to attain to the highest prizes in the Service, while if they prove decidedly incompetent, or incurably indolent, they must expect to be removed from it.

The first step towards carrying this principle into effect should be, the establishment of a proper system of examination before appointment, which should be followed, as at present, by a short period of probation. The necessity of this has been so far admitted that some kind of examination does now take place before clerks are admitted into any of the following offices: — The Treasury, the Colonial Office, the Board of Trade, the Privy Council Office, the Poor Law Board, the War Office, the Ordnance Office, the Audit Office, the Paymaster General's

Office, the Inland Revenue Office, the Emigration Office, and some others . . .

The preliminary examination of candidates for civil employment, however, cannot be conducted in an effective and consistent manner throughout the Service, while it is left to each department to determine the nature of the examination and to examine the candidates . . .

We accordingly recommend that a central Board should be constituted for conducting the examination of all candidates for the public service whom it may be thought right to subject to such a test. Such board should be composed of men holding an independent position, and capable of commanding general confidence . . . persons experienced in the education of the youth of the upper and middle classes, and persons who are familiar with the conduct of official business . . .

We are of opinion that this examination should be in all cases a competing literary examination. This ought not to exclude careful previous inquiry into the age, health, and moral fitness of the candidates . . . We see no other mode by which (in the case of inferior no less than of superior offices) the double object can be attained of selecting the fittest person, and of avoiding the evils of patronage.

For the superior situations endeavours should be made to secure the services of the most promising young men of the day, by a competing examination on a level with the highest description of education in this country. In this class of situations there is no limit to the demands which may ultimately be made upon the abilities of those who, entering them simply as junior clerks, gradually rise to the highest posts in them . . .

It would be desirable to retain the probation as at present, rendering it more efficient by precise reports of the conduct of the probationers.

In the examinations which we have recommended, we consider that the right of competing should be open to all persons, of a given age . .

With regard to the age of admission, we are of opinion that in the case of candidates for superior situations the limits should, as a general rule, be 19 and 25; in the case of candidates for inferior offices, 17 and 21 . . .

As we have already spoken of the importance of establishing a proper distinction between intellectual and mechanical labour, we need offer no further observations on this most vital point . . . We consider that a great step has been taken by the appointment in several offices of a class of supplementary clerks, receiving uniform salaries in each department, and capable therefore of being transferred, without inconvenience, from one to another, according as the demand for their services may be greater or less at any particular time; and we expect that the moveable character of this class of officers, and superior standard of examination which we have proposed for the higher class, will together have the effect of marking the distinction between them in a proper manner . . .

Now, setting aside cases of actual favouritism, there must be many instances in which the chief permanent officers fail to perceive, and properly to bring into notice, the valuable qualities of those beneath them . . . All such cases are watched with jealousy even now, and if promotion by seniority were wholly set aside, without the introduction of propersafeguards, they would be the cause of still more discomfort.

It ought, therefore, to be a leading object with the Government so to regulate promotion by merit as to provide every possible security against its abuse . . .

Upon a review of the recommendations contained in this paper it will be seen that the objects which we have principally in view are these:

1. To provide, by a proper system of examination, for the supply of the public service with a thoroughly efficient class of men.

2. To encourage industry and foster merit, by teaching all public servants to look forward to promotion according to their deserts, and to expect the highest prizes in the service if they can qualify themselves for them.

3. To mitigate the evils which result from the fragmentary character of the Service, and to introduce into it some elements of unity, by placing the first appointments upon a uniform footing, opening the way to the promotion of public officers to staff appointments in other departments than their own, and introducing into the lower ranks a body of men (the supplementary clerks) whose services may be made available

at any time in any office whatever.

It remains for us to express our conviction that if any change of the importance of those which we have recommended is to be carried into effect, it can only be successfully done through the medium of an Act of Parliament. The existing system is supported by long usage and powerful interests; and were any Government to introduce material alterations into it, in consequence of their own convictions, without taking the precaution to give those alterations the force of law, it is almost certain that they would be imperceptibly, or perhaps avowedly, abandoned by their successors, if they were not even allowed to fall into disuse by the very Government which had originated them. A few clauses would accomplish all that is proposed in this paper, and it is our firm belief that a candid statement of the grounds of the measure would insure its success and popularity in the country, and would remove many misconceptions which are now prejudicial to the public service.

Organisation of the permanent civil service, 23 November 1853, *Parliamentary Papers*, HC 1854, xxvii [1713], pp. 3-23.

24 The Response

Given the long-established patterns of recruitment for posts in government departments, it was hardly unexpected that obstructive attitudes were to be found there when the Northcote-Trevelyan proposals became known and that resistance to its recommendations persisted for many years. The Treasury circulated the Report to a number of leading educationalists and senior civil servants. Their responses were collected together and printed. In general, the former group welcomed the proposals as a healthy stimulus to improved standards of education in both schools and universities. On the other hand, even the most reforming civil servants felt the scheme went too far. Inspired by a desire for economy and efficiency, Gladstone believed that the reforms would in fact ease the way in which the sons of the upper classes might secure posts in the civil service and had been encouraged in this view by Trevelyan.

(a) W.E. GLADSTONE

I do not hesitate to say that one of the great recommendations of the change in my eyes would be its tendency to strengthen and multiply the ties between the higher classes and the possession of administrative power. As a member for Oxford, I look forward eagerly to its operation. There, happily, we are not without some lights of experience to throw upon this part of the subject. The objection which I always hear there from persons who wish to retain restrictions upon elections is this: 'If you leave them to examination, Eton, Harrow, Rugby, and the other public schools will carry *everything*.' I have a strong impression that the aristocracy of this country are even superior in natural gifts, on the average, to the mass: but it is plain that with their acquired advantages, their *insensible* education, irrespective of book-learning, they have an immense superiority. This applies in its degree to all those who may be called gentlemen by birth and training; and it must be remembered that an essential part of any such plan as is now under discussion is the separation of *work*, wherever it can be made, into mechanical and intellectual, a separation which will open to the highly educated class a career and give them a command over all the higher parts of the civil service, which up to this time they have never enjoyed.

W.E. Gladstone to Lord John Russell, January 1854

(b) SIR JAMES STEPHEN

Stephen, for long associated with the Colonial Office, had entered the Civil Service from the Bar.

The patrons of these clerkships — that is, the principal ministers of the Crown — are themselves so ill remunerated, that those high trusts are practically confined to persons born to ample fortunes. No one else can afford to undertake them. The consequent narrowness of the range of choice is, I apprehend, a serious evil. But the range of choice will become still more narrow, and the evil yet more serious, if the remuneration of these great offices be further reduced, by depriving the holders of them of all their most valuable patronage. It is said, indeed, that they regard it as a burden, not as an advantage. I can only answer that I never yet served under any Secretary of State who did not, at least, appear to attach a very high interest indeed to the power of giving such places to his dependents and his friends . . .

I am of opinion that the contemplated Act of Parliament ought not to be passed, and that the plan of electing to all vacancies in the Public Service the candidates who shall pass the best examinations ought not to take effect. In order to provide a remedy for the evils which did exist in my time, and which, as I suppose, exist still, it would, I apprehend, be sufficient to subject each nominee to an examination to be conducted by strangers to the Government — by men of indisputable learning and integrity — who should admit every candidate who attained the standard of skill and knowledge prescribed for this particular branch of the Service, and who should reject every candidate who fell below that standard.

On reading over what I have written, I see that I have omitted to call your attention to the almost incalculable magnitude of the political changes which the proposed abdication of all the patronage of the Crown in the Public Offices must invoke, and to the seeming rashness of plunging at once into such deep and dark waters, without first making a tentative, experimental, and partial entrance into them.

Reorganisation of the civil service, *Parliamentary Papers*, HC 1854-55, xx [1870], 79-80.

(c) R.R.W. LINGEN

Secretary to the Committee of Council for Education and well aware of the deficiencies within existing government departments.

The first and cardinal quality that you want is a deep self-sacrificing sense of duty; not a conventional one, satisfied by doing and avoiding certain prescribed or proscribed things; but such as is only satisfied when it has done its best, whether the sacrifice demanded thereby be that of ease, personal feeling, or private opinion. This sense of duty is one of the quietest and least demonstrative of qualities, because it finds much of its reward in itself. You cannot go into the general market and lay your hand upon it as a visible commodity. If you would select men with direct reference to it, there is no other criterion of it than personal knowledge, no other method of introducing it, *suo nomine*, than that of personal selection. But if, in the Public Service, personal selection cannot be trusted, and you are driven by its abuse into the necessity of discovering some more disinterested method, then you must be content to select men with reference to those palpable qualities in connexion with which a high sense of duty is the most commonly found. And for this purpose, perhaps, no criterion is more generally available than thorough mastery over some one field of knowledge. I would neither favour nor exclude any particular field. What you want is, not the knowledge, but the evidence of qualities which the acquisition of it affords. He who has mastered any one branch of liberal knowledge, must have toiled through details as uninteresting *per se* as the smallest of those in an office, and must have learnt how to measure the worth of parts by that of the whole which each contributes to form.

And here I must say, that I think you lay far too much stress upon the adaptation of previous knowledge to particular offices, and upon the distinction between interesting and uninteresting work.

There are very few of the higher permanent officers who would find themselves much aided in their work by a subordinate who expatiated on the general question, or who became lifeless over the routine of business. The knowledge of a department is picked up quietly within it — much of the work called mechanical has only become so because some good administrator has seen how to stereotype the method; the particular act (of filling up the form, etc) may be mechanical, but all such things have their lesson for those who will attend to them; and, in fact, the interest of almost all work depends not so much upon its nature, as upon the degree in which it is mastered and comprehended . . .

A main point in the organisation of the Service, in my opinion, is gradually to abolish all the situations under £300 a year which are now held by persons on the superior establishments of offices; to delegate the whole of the work now done by these gentlemen to a class who, beginning at £80 or £100, shall rise to £300 or £400 as a maximum, being analogous to the clerks of merchants, bankers, or actuaries; to reduce the higher class of offices very greatly in number, and to make the lowest appointment to it begin at not less than £300 per annum. The Board of Examiners would see that the tests were made proportionate to the duties and emoluments of office in each of the two grades.

I agree with your remarks as to the rules of augmentation within each class, and of promotion from class to class, except that I see no practical use in your register, and would merely make it a rule that, on every increase of salary or promotion, the parliamentary chief of the department should be bound to call for, and to record, the observations of the permanent head of the department, and also those of the officer under whom the one advanced in salary, or promoted to a higher grade had immediately been serving. This would not be worth much as a guarantee for merit, but it would occasionally check any serious abuse.

The Public Offices are, in general, very ill arranged as regards construction. The rooms are far too numerous for the purposes of ready reference and supervision. The principle of construction, in my opinion, should be, to make large halls for the main body of the clerks, with side-rooms opening out of them for a few superior officers. I have seen vast premises of business in the City, where the same principle has been successfully maintained under the necessity of building in many stories. In my own department there are sixty persons (including messengers and copying clerks) scattered on four different floors, throughout twenty-five separate rooms.

Ibid., pp. 101-6.

(d) EDWARD ROMILLY

Chairman of the Board of Audit, provided the Treasury with five papers written at different times. In general he feared that the recommendations would result in 'a democratical Civil Service, side by side with an aristocratical Legislature'. This piece was actually written in 1848.

But is it so certain that public offices are paid too much? May not the real evil be that they do too little? If it should turn out on inquiry that the Civil Service is not on the best footing, and that its officers are not as efficient as they ought to be, will matters be mended by merely reducing their numbers? If the present staff be inadequate from incompetency to carry on the public business, will half that same incompetent staff succeed better? The truth is that we are beginning at the wrong end. Our establishments should first be made efficient, and then they may be reduced or rather, they will reduce themselves. Mere reductions and consolidation of offices will do but little; they will not even effect any real economy. A certain number of the inefficient may be squeezed out of the service, but a large amount of inactivity and dissatisfaction will be left behind. The work to be done will be more imperfectly done than before; and though its cost may be less, the object for which it has been incurred will be as far off as ever. The truth is, that few persons have seriously turned their thoughts to the real evil. The expedient of cutting down establishments and reducing salaries is periodically resorted to; and it never occurs to these economists, whether it would not be more to the purpose to lay down and enforce rules by which our public establishments may be made permanently efficient.

Ibid., pp. 273-4.

(e) GEORGE ARBUTHNOT

Auditor of the Civil List and strongest defender of the existing civil service.

The proposal for the separation of the intellectual from mechanical labour is to some extent mixed up with the views stated in the Report condemnatory of the departmental system. It is true that in most offices there is a large amount of mere copying work, which when not of a confidential character may be entrusted with advantage to an inferior class of clerks. It is a matter of discretion to what extent recourse ought to be had to this description of assistance. In some few departments, also, the duties of the administrative or directing functionaries are so distinct from those of the clerks who carry into effect the routine duties, that the line of demarcation is easily drawn. But in the great mass of the Revenue departments a thorough acquaintance with forms is so essential to a full comprehension of the business to be carried on, that to fulfil the superior offices satisfactorily a previous apprenticeship in the inferior classes is essential. In order to direct details effectively, an officer ought to know how to do them himself. In order to become acquainted with technical or legal phraseology, the young clerk must begin by copying documents. As in professional pursuits, the efficient Civil Servant is formed by making him in the first instance a good workmen. The most distinguished officers of this class commenced early in life at the drudgery of the desk. It is upon this principle that the system of promotion which has worked so well in the Customs has been established, and the value of the theory which would disturb that system has yet to be tested.

Ibid., p. 412.

25 A More General View

SIR ARTHUR HELPS

Helps's career in the civil service was to be very varied. An extremely able administrator, he was brought in as Bathurst's successor as Clerk to the Privy Council in 1860, at the time that Office acquired public health functions. He served as Commissioner for Relief in Ireland during the famine.

Objects of Government

In the first place, let us be careful not to limit too much the objects of government. Governments in past ages having interfered so much, and often so unwisely, has given us a peculiar distaste for what we call government interference, and has made men contented to accept a very low view of the objects and purposes of government. But government is not merely police. It is something personal; it has a representative character; its business is not confined to the care of life and property; it has in fact some national part to play in the world, some great character to sustain. In short, it seems to me that the just idea of government is not fulfilled unless it acts with the greatness of soul and the extent of insight and foresight of the best men in the state, and with the power of the whole body, in those matters which cannot be accomplished by individual exertion. Now this is what many a man expresses unconsciously when he exclaims 'The government should undertake this great work; should reward this eminent man, promote that discovery, encourage that art'; or words to that effect. He means that the government should express the wisdom and gratitude of the best part of the nation in a way which that part could not do or ought not to be expected to do, by its own individual exertion . . .

One of the first things for a government is self-preservation . . . Now this care for self-preservation on the part of government, may seem to be a selfish thing and likely to lead to mere repressiveness and inactivity; but these are not the means by which I consider that self-preservation will ever be effected. On the contrary, I believe that if governors and people in authority really understood human nature, they would perceive that some judicious activity on their part is the only thing which can give life to their institutions . . . But the object of a government should be to breed up the men under it to do with less and less of it, or so to extend its action, that if its interference and control are not diminished, it is only because its sphere of usefulness is enlarged. People in authority should understand that government must be a thing of growth; must attend to, if not comprehend, the future . . .

Mode and means of government

. . . The form for instance of a Cabinet and many of the Cabinet arrangements for business in this country, are the result of much adaptation, and could not easily be amended. It is obvious that in every form of government considerable attention should be paid to the distribution of functions amongst the great officers of state; and that care must be taken to make the functions of these officers grow and change with the growth and fluctuation of the affairs of the country. In our own country the great officers of state are too few . . . the present duties of the Home Secretary might be divided, I think, with great advantage . . . Does any one who knows anything about the subject, doubt of there being enough business in the Colonial Office to employ any two of the greatest minds in the country as chiefs of that department?

. . . What is wanted is to bring more intellectual power within command of the heads of departments, and moreover that this power should neither be elicited in a hostile manner, nor on the other hand that it should be too subservient . . .

Friends in Council (London, 1861), ii, 64-7, 81-3.

V

A New Era
in Government:
the 1870s and 1880s

Although the Civil Service Commission was established in
May 1855, and it began to organize examinations for
nominated candidates, open competitive examination for entry
into the Civil Service was not introduced until the Order in
Council of 1870. Even then, the Home and Foreign Offices were
excluded. The Order was extended by Treasury arrangements
for two levels of examination. The first was designed for
university graduates seeking the higher posts and the second
for the lower posts available. Thus the two most important
recommendations in the Northcote-Trevelyan Report were
implemented and the way lay open for the development of an
efficient and professional civil service. Difficulties within
departments had resulted in the employment of what were
known as 'copying clerks'. The 1870s saw the appointment of
the Playfair Commission to investigate the structure and make
recommendations for grading the civil service as a whole. The
1860s had seen the strengthening of political parties both
within and without Parliament. Reliable majorities could allow
governments to introduce innovatory legislation with a reasonable chance of success. Government departments found
themselves hard worked and in need of more staff. Pressure on
parliamentary time was forcing changes in procedure and
encouraging greater administrative discretion.

26 The System of 'Copying Clerks'

Whatever may be the merits of such a system when applied to
offices in which the number of extra clerks is very large in
proportion to that of the established clerks, in consequence of

the work being liable to large fluctuations, we doubt whether it would be equally applicable to offices where this is not the case. In such Departments as the Treasury, or the Home, Foreign, and Colonial Offices, the maintenance of a large body of extra clerks would soon lead to abuses. Men who looked to rise to the highest posts would have to enter the service as extra clerks, and those of them who failed to gain situations on the establishment would become discontented with their position, and would be continually urging the claims of the supplementary clerks to further advantages.

From the various statements which have been laid before us, and of which the general results will be found in the Appendix, we have come to the conclusion that the maintenance of two distinct orders of clerks in the same office must, in the great majority of cases, lead to difficulties and embarrassments which cannot easily or permanently be surmounted. Every improvement in the qualifications of the supplementary clerks tends to render the distinction between them and the established clerks more odious and untenable, so long as all are equally borne on the books of the same Department; and every privilege which is conceded to the supplementary clerks in one office leads to demands for corresponding privileges in other offices, and increases the temptation to make unsuitable appointments from too high a class . . .

Observing then, as we do, that the system of attaching supplementary clerks to the establishment of each office does not obviate the necessity of employing a considerable number of law stationers' clerks, and other temporary assistants, and that it has an obvious tendency to produce confusion and dissatisfaction within the offices to which it is applied, we are led to consider whether the advantages which it was expected to produce may not be better attained in another manner . . .

We propose, therefore, that the distinction between established and supplementary clerks in the several departments be abandoned; that no more appointments be made to the supplementary classes; and that they be allowed gradually to die out, unless it be thought desirable and found possible to transfer any portion of the men at once to the department of which we are about to speak.

We further propose that a central copying office be

established, under the control of a superintending officer, to which the several public departments may make application from time to time for as many writers as may be required . . .

We will only add, therefore, that we are of opinion that should such a copying office be contemplated, it would, on many accounts, be convenient to attach it to the office of the Civil Service Commissioners. Their acquaintance with the young men who offer themselves as candidates for Civil Service appointments, the facilities which they have for conducting examinations, keeping registers, and managing the machinery which would be required for working the plan proposed, point them out as the best persons for undertaking its superintendence. One or more officers would of course be required for the special conduct of the business; and we would propose that these should be attached to the Commissioners' establishment.

It is to be expected that this plan, if successfully carried into operation, will not only relieve the Government of a great deal of embarrassment with regard to the position of the supplementary clerks, but will ultimately render the establishments of the several public offices more efficient for their purpose at a much less cost than the present.

Report on the Employment of Supplemental and Temporary Clerks in the Civil Service, *Parliamentary Papers*, HC 1865 xxx, (251), 2-4.

27 A Retiring Civil Servant's View of the Job

SIR ARTHUR HELPS

Helps had been private secretary to a Chancellor of the Exchequer, Commissioner of Claims and became Clerk to the Privy Council in 1860. He was writing at the close of his career. (See extract 25.)

Another point to be carefully watched in the conduct of business is, not to confuse rules with principles, and especially, that no man should needlessly lay down rules which may hamper himself. His principles may be ever so strict: the rules he lays down should be very elastic, and certainly he should not be prone to communicate to others, needlessly, those rules which he may have instituted as guides to himself. Hence, in making communications upon the subject of the business alluded to, it is seldom wise to say, 'We never do this, or that, or the other — it is contrary to our rules, or our practice'. Perhaps, in a few weeks or months, there may come a case in which it is necessary to violate the rule, or depart from the practice; and then there is an appearance of lamentable inconsistency. The circumstances and conditions of life in any community, where high civilization prevails, are so numerous, various, and difficult to be imagined, even by men of fertile imaginations, that no prudent man shuts himself up in rules made by himself, like a silkworm winding itself up in its own cocoon.

Then there is the general correspondence about the matter to be considered. Herein there must be much continuity of aim and purpose, and, therefore, clearness of expression. If we could trace up some of the greatest errors to their source, we should probably find, that many a decision which has failed to decide, and has, indeed, failed to convey its exact meaning in any way, has been thus made inefficient by its language, in some of the principal sentences, being thorough patchwork: designed by one man; corrected by another; revised by a third, while some little point, merely of diction, has at the last been interlineated by a fourth. The final drawing of any important document should be one man's work, embodying the various corrections made by other men's minds, but having that unity and force which can only be the outcome of a single mind.

Another important point in the transaction of business, and especially in such a case as I have been considering, is to divide the subject-matter into several sections. One of the chief arts in mastering any subject consists in subdivision. It is an art which presupposes the existence of method. In a previous chapter on education, I was able to make only a few suggestions as to how this supreme effort of division and classification, called method, could be taught. It is a thing, however, of inestimable value, and must, somehow or other, be acquired by any man who has to deal promptly with business of much pressure and magnitude. Referring to the case in question, there may be scores of arguments applying to different sections of the case. If these arguments are left as separate forces, as it were, and are not brought, as a mathematician would say, to 'resultants' in their respective sections, the man who has to decide wanders about in a jungle of unsettled thought, and is perpetually taking up his facts and arguments at wrong times, in the course of forming his determination. Whereas, if the various facts and arguments had been brought to their conclusions in their respective sections, the Minister's labour, in coming to a determination upon the whole subject, would have been almost indefinitely facilitated.

Thoughts upon Government (London, 1872), pp. 206-9.

28 The 1870 Order in Council

The 1860s had seen the general adoption of various types of limited competition for places in the civil service. A Select Committee in 1860 had suggested that from time to time departments should follow the example of the India Office in 1859 and experiment with open competition. In late 1869 Robert Lowe appealed to Gladstone: 'As I have so often tried in vain, will you bring the question of the civil service before the cabinet today? Something must be decided. We cannot keep matters in this discreditable state of abeyance.' The Prime Minister steered open competition through a divided cabinet by suggesting that it should only be introduced into those departments where the minister agreed.

(a) GLADSTONE'S VIEW

. . . The administrative changes, as my hon. Friend defines them are very considerable, although the principle upon which he proposes we should act in making them at first sight looks simple enough. The general idea which Members conceive is, that first appointments in the Civil Service are to be regulated by open competition — the correlative principle having been long ago established — namely, that promotions in the Civil Service are regulated by the Chiefs of Departments, and are understood and believed to be given — and, I am bound to say, are given — under the influence of merit and service alone. But when we pass beyond these general statements there are very important matters of detail to consider. There is that which of itself amounts to a complete reorganization of the Civil Service — the division proposed to be introduced and which I hope will be carried out as far as possible, and made as clear as possible, between duties which are mechanical and formal, and those duties which require high mental training. That is a question which cannot be decided by rule of thumb; it cannot be disposed of by laying down a strict and absolute principle for all the Departments, but it requires of necessity a careful examination into the circumstances of each Department; and the precise point at which the line is to be drawn is a matter that cannot be settled except in detail and after minute scrutiny. There are other matters to be considered in establishing the principle of open competition. For example, it will be necessary that the responsible officers of the Government should reserve in a very strict and clear manner, so as to preclude all possibility of mistake, the power of defining and determining, from time to time, what are those superior offices which are to be considered as Staff appointments, and to which persons may be introduced and appointed irrespective of any prior services they may have rendered in the Civil Departments. That is a matter of the utmost consequence, and one on which, when once open competition is established, it is necessary the clearest understanding should prevail; because those who come into the Civil Service upon the basis of open competition, determined only by merit, may be disposed to rate highly, and perhaps justly so, their own claims to the fulfilment of what they may consider a covenant with respect to prospective advancement. We must, therefore, consider carefully the terms of that covenant, so as to reserve in the hands of the Government that discretion with respect to the higher appointments which it is absolutely necessary for the public service they should retain. Both, therefore, with respect to the limit, upwards, of those offices the first appointments to which need not be, and could not be, the subject of open competition; and, again, with respect to the limit, downwards, of all that class of offices with regard to which a test examination applies, and a rate of pay governed by what the market requires, much has to be considered . . . I can venture to say, unless our present expectations are very much disappointed, it will be within a limited period in our power to announce the establishment of a system of open competition upon an extended scale, a scale quite sufficient, even if there should be exceptions, to enable the public to test its principle in a perfect scale, and determine upon the propriety of applying it to any cases that may remain with greater advantage than we may be said to possess at this moment . . . I think no lengthened period will elapse before it will have assumed a practical shape.

Hansard, 3rd series, cxcix, 812-15, 25 February 1870.

(b) THE ORDER

. . . Except as herein-after is excepted, all appointments which it may be necessary to make, after the 31st day of August next, to any of the situations included or to be included in Schedule A to this Order annexed, shall be made by means of competitive examinations, according to regulations to be from time to time framed by the said Civil Service Commissioners, and approved by the Commissioners of Her Majesty's Treasury, open to all Persons (of the requisite age, health, character, and other qualifications prescribed in the said regulations) who may be desirous of attending the same, subject to the payment of such fees as the said Civil Service Commissioners . . . may from time to time require; such examinations to be held at such periods, and for such situations, . . . as the said Civil Service Commissioners, . . . shall from time to time determine.

Order in Council, 4 June 1870, *Parliamentary Papers*, HC 1875 xxiii [C.113.I], Appendix C, p. 243.

29 The Emergence of the 'Treasury Grades'

Pressure of business continued to increase the need for supplementary clerks for routine duties. Robert Lowe attempted to regularise the practice by issuing an Order in Council on 19 August 1871 which deemed these writers to be unestablished clerks paid at a uniform rate and without sick pay or leave arrangements. Resulting discontent provoked the appointment of a Select Committee in 1873 to investigate the problem. On the recommendation of that Committee, two-thirds of the temporary staff became permanent and therefore gained pension rights. The problem remained. There had been no resolution of the debate on division of labour or how, if the principle were to be accepted, it should be effected. In the hope that comprehensive reorganization might be possible, a Commission of Inquiry under the chairmanship of Dr Lyon Playfair was appointed in 1874 to investigate the organization of the civil service. The membership of the Playfair Commission was unusual in that it included six heads of departments and only two members of Parliament. The evidence collected by the Commission provides a detailed picture of civil service practice and personnel in the 1870s. The report wholeheartedly supported the division of labour, the use of open competition and a service in which staff could move easily from one department to another. Despite the weight of evidence and official support for the Playfair recommendations, few changes were in fact made. Stafford Northcote, now Chancellor of the Exchequer, advised against 'precipitate action'. An Order in Council of 1876 included some of the Commission's proposals. It created the Lower Division of the civil service which was to be constituted of men and boys 'engaged to serve in any department of the State to which they may, from time to time, be appointed or transferred'. But the condition was only to apply to new recruits. No Lower Division clerk could hope to earn more than £350 a year. Provision was also made for the employment of men or boy writers for copying. The only comment on the Higher Division related to promotion. Its existence appeared to be assumed. The emergence of a uniform service was still some way off and the Treasury in no way discouraged discrepancies between departments. By the time the Ridley Commission was appointed in 1886, it was clear that the principles of open competition and division of labour were generally accepted. The open competition or examinations were no longer seen as experimental. The Commissioners were concerned to work out further details of the application of division of labour. Their work appears much more like that of the Civil Service Inquiry Commissioners to come later than like that of their predecessors faced with the problem of pressing a new style of organization certain to rouse hostile opposition. They saw their job as one of clearing up difficulties which had emerged in the last few years, — the numbers of staff in the different grades, salaries, hours, pensions, organization of offices. They emphasized that the division between the Higher and Lower Divisions had been set too low.

Most of the tidying up operation suggested by the Ridley Commissioners was effected by Orders in Council in 1890.

The division of labour is therefore, as experience shows, beset with difficulties. It is nevertheless, in our opinion, the key of the position.

The amount of simple routine work in the bulk of public Offices is very great in proportion to the amount of work of a higher class. The mechanical and monotonous labour on which Clerks must, under such circumstances, be so long and continuously employed, in Offices where no division, or an inadequate division, of labour exists, does not, by any means, as a matter of course, fit them for discharging the duties of those higher posts in the Service which involve responsibility, discretion, and power to direct work, and to deal with the outside public in such a manner as to uphold the credit and efficiency of their Departments. It need hardly be pointed out that having regard to the limited number of these higher posts, it would be a great waste of power to require that all the Clerks employed in the Service should have received a sufficiently liberal education to fit them to fill such posts with efficiency. But even those so fitted in the first instance, unless, from some exceptional circumstances, they have, at an early period of their career, had work given to them which develops their powers, are apt to degenerate into mere machines, and become incapable of the exercise of higher qualities. The routine work in which they have been so long engaged, and with which they are so familiar, appears to them to be the end instead of being merely the means to the end. They cannot distinguish and separate the substance from the form in which it has always been presented to their minds, and the result is that a large number of the general body of Clerks are not qualified to fill efficiently the higher posts in the service.

Another consequence of not distinguishing work of an inferior kind from the more important work of the Service, is the discontent to which it leads. Although, as we have said elsewhere, the pay of the Clerks in the Civil Service, as a whole, compares favourably with that of Clerks in private employ, the former in many large offices suffer under a real evil in the slowness of promotion which is the necessary consequence of very large numbers in the lower, as compared with the higher classes, all having a presumptive right to rise to the classes above them, and few of them having any real prospect of doing so. This is, in our opinion, the real grievance of the Service, and it can only be met either by paying extravagantly for inferior work, which is, of course, out of the question, or by distinguishing the work and pay so that the mass of the inferior work may be entrusted to a class of men to whom comparatively low salaries will be an object, and so that all those who do superior work may have a fair prospect of increase of pay and promotion.

Unless, therefore, some division of labour and of pay can be effected, it is impossible to establish either any general system for testing efficiency, or any system of pay or promotion which will stimulate and reward efficiency, or remove grounds for discontent.

It appears to us that, under these circumstances, there is no other possible way, if due regard be paid both to the economy and the efficiency of the public service, of providing for the range of work which exists in public Offices, than by making a distinction between those classes of Clerks who do the higher and more responsible work, and those who do the inferior work. To carry this out under a system of open competition, it is necessary that there should be, as we have proposed above, two separate and distinct schemes of examination for admission to the public service, and two separate and distinct grades of Clerks, the comparative numbers in such grades varying widely, of course, in different Offices, according to the character of the work of each. To each of these grades, certain service rates of pay should be attached throughout the public service, and persons should be appointed on the distinct understanding that they have no claim to go beyond the maximum of the service salary of the grade in which they are placed, and that any further advancement must depend on special official aptitude. Clerks in the Lower Division, of which the work will be uniform throughout the Service, should also understand distinctly that they are to serve in any office under the State where they may be wanted.

Beyond these two grades of Clerks there would be Staff appointments, including such officers as Chief Clerks and

Principal Clerks, of which the number and pay should be fixed with reference to the work of each Department. The selection of men to fill these offices should be left entirely to the Heads of each Department, with the full understanding that, within the office, merit and not seniority is the condition for selection, and that recourse may, if necessary, be had to the outside world. The responsible Head of a Department has so strong an individual interest in having these appointments efficiently filled, that he is not likely to abuse this power, even if it be optional with him to appoint to such offices from outside the Service. As pointed out by Sir Louis Mallet in his evidence, any thoroughly competent man already in an office has a great advantage over an outsider, and is certain to get his due. It might be well, however, that all Staff appointments should be included in an Order in Council.

The rate of remuneration to be fixed for the Lower Division of Clerks should only exceed the rate fixed for similar work in the open market by such an amount as will attract to the public service the *élite* of the class employed on similar work outside of it, that is, the *élite* of that class of persons by whom such situations would be valued as offering them better pay than they could otherwise obtain. An excessive rate of pay for such work, more especially when admission to the public service is regulated by open competition, attracts men of a class employed generally upon higher work outside, and men who are capable of performing much better work than that required of them. Such men, finding their position fall short of their expectations, are not the most efficient agents for the performance of the work they have to do. Too often they either become disheartened and lose their energies altogether, or devote them to matters outside of the Service, or to an agitation for levelling up their salaries to those of some other Department in which the rates are higher. Nor is this to be wondered at. They know that their own salaries are not fixed with reference to the work which they have to do, measured by the salaries paid in the open market, and they see no reason why they should not be paid as well as the highest paid Departments, in which, presumably, the rates of salary have as little relation to the character of the work as in their own.

With these views we think that the salaries of the Lower

Division should commence at £80, and rise by triennial increments to £200. Beyond this there should be a few places in each office, with duty pay not exceeding £100 a year, which may be given to Clerks in this Lower Division, if they have special aptitude, thus conferring on them a rank like that of non-commissioned officers. These increments and this duty pay should be given in the same manner and on the same conditions as the service scale increments, and duty pay in the Higher Divisions, as detailed below.

We have taken a good deal of evidence respecting Boy Clerks, from which it appears that their employment, under proper supervision, is both desirable and economical. In every office there is some work which can be done by boys as efficiently as by men. The experience of the Civil Service Commissioners, as described in the evidence, is that a very ordinary boy, early in his career, will do more than half a man's work, while he can be got for less than half a man's wages, and that the best boys will do more than an average man's work. The aptitude, moreover, which he gains while a Boy Clerk, renders him at once valuable to an office when he succeeds in obtaining the position of a Man Clerk. We, therefore, propose that the Lower Division should embrace a class of boys, a limited number of whom should be promoted to be Clerks after approved good service, those not so promoted being discharged on attaining their nineteenth year of age. The manner in which these boys should be selected and promoted we have explained in answer to the first question.

The whole of our proposals on this part of the subject are based on the assumption that the Lower Division is recruited strictly as we suggest. Any attempt to recruit this Division from such men as form the main body of Civil Service Writers would result in the collapse of the whole scheme we have recommended; though, as we state hereafter, we do not doubt that among the Writers there do exist men who would be well fitted for the new body. But we cannot too strongly state our conviction that, to a large extent, the efficiency of the Public Service will depend upon this Lower Division being recruited from the men whom the proposed terms of service will attract in the open market. Not only is the efficiency of this Division, in itself, a matter of the gravest importance, but is also affects most seriously the constitution and numbers of the Higher

Division. Unless the Lower Division is able to take a large proportion of the work now done by Established Clerks, our scheme would be unjustifiably extravagant.

First Report of the Civil Service Inquiry Commission, *Parliamentary Papers*, HC 1875 [c. 1113], pp.14-15.

30 The Problem of Parliamentary Time

One of the greatest parliamentary difficulties for governments in the 1870s was the inadequacy of time for the conduct of business. The emergence of stronger cabinets with reliable voting support in the Commons and the ever-increasing pressure from different groups for executive activity resulted in more proposed legislation and created difficulties in the management of parliamentary business. The conventions of Commons procedure strictly limited the time available for government business to two days in any week. The session itself was short, usually lasting from just after Christmas until the beginning of August. After the first few weeks negotiations would begin between ministers and the House in general to permit encroachments on the time normally reserved for private business or to approve morning sittings. Time also had to be found for the granting of supply. The financial reforms of the 1860s had removed some of the need to discuss individual votes in the committee of supply, but in the place of wrangles over detailed estimates were to be found extended discussions of departmental policy. It was these difficulties which were to lead to the introduction of much tighter rules of procedure especially in the committee of supply and to the greater use of administrative discretion.

(a) NEGOTIATION

MOTION

PARLIAMENT — ARRANGEMENT OF PUBLIC BUSINESS

The CHANCELLOR of the EXCHEQUER, in moving —
'That the Orders of the Day subsequent to the Army

Discipline and Regulation Bill be postponed until after the Notice of Motion for leave to bring in a Bill for promoting University Education in Ireland;' said, he made the Motion in accordance with a promise which he had given the other evening to the hon. Member for Roscommon (the O'Conor Don), which was partly dictated by the consideration that the Government, by fixing a Bill of their own for a Morning Sitting, had prevented him from bringing forward his Bill on the occasion on which he would otherwise have done so. He (the Chancellor of the Exchequer) wished to take that opportunity of saying that the business-like spirit in which the Army Discipline and Regulation Bill had been discussed encouraged the Government to hope that they would be able to make further progress with that measure that night; and he trusted that the House might be disposed to allow them to take a Morning Sitting tomorrow, in order to go on with it, so that they might, if possible, get it through Committee before the House rose for the Whitsuntide Holidays.

Mr NEWDEGATE asked the Chancellor of the Exchequer when he intended to take the Customs and Inland Revenue Bill? The House was aware that he had a Notice of some importance to be considered before the second reading of that Bill. He would also like to know when it was proposed to take the Criminal Code (Indictable Offences) Bill? At present it stood for Tuesday next, but it appeared to him impossible that the Government should propose to go on with it before the Whitsuntide Recess.

Mr KNATCHBULL-HUGESSEN said, that having balloted with praise-worthy perseverance during the Session, he had obtained first place tomorrow for his Motion on the subject of Brewers' Licences, and he thought it rather hard that at the very last moment Notice of a Morning Sitting should be given, which placed him at a disadvantage. He hoped the Government would take steps to make and keep a House at the Evening Sitting.

Sir JULIÁN GOLDSMID called attention to the fact that it was only at the last moment the Government informed the House that they proposed to hold a Morning Sitting; and he would ask the Chancellor of the Exchequer whether, in future, it would not be possible for him to give some longer and more formal Notice with reference to the intention of the Government to hold Morning Sittings?

Sir ALEXANDER GORDON hoped the Government would not put down the Army Discipline and Regulation Bill for the Morning Sitting. This was a Bill in which he had several important Amendments to propose; and as he was also a Member of the Parliamentary Reporting Committee which would meet at 12 o'clock to draw up their Report, and this was also a subject in which he took a great interest, he trusted the Government would not then take the Army Discipline and Regulation Bill.

Mr E. JENKINS seconded the appeal of the hon. and gallant Gentleman, and pointed out the inconsistency of the reasons advanced by the Government for these Morning Sittings. Last year the Government excused themselves for taking early Morning Sittings because of the opposition offered to the Mutiny Bill. This year they appeared to ask for it because of the business-like way in which the House had carried through the Business. Therefore, whether they opposed or facilitated Business, the Government seemed equally determined to have Morning Sittings.

Mr A. MILLS considered the Army Discipline and Regulation Bill of much more importance than the question of Parliamentary Reporting, and he trusted the Chancellor of the Exchequer would proceed with it. He had himself a Notice of the Paper for tomorrow evening, but would willingly sacrifice it in order to promote Public Business.

Hansard, 3rd series, ccxlvi, 403-5; 15 May 1879.

(b) OBSTRUCTION

The early 1880s saw intensive obstruction by Irish members of Commons business and the introduction of important new rules of procedure in 1882. These rules have been described by Edward Hughes as 'the real watershed between the ancient parliamentary régime and modern practice'. In effect, the government could now claim four 'Government nights' a week and hold in reserve new powers for closing a debate. The Irish obstruction had brought the long-standing problem to a head, as Gladstone explained when he introduced the resolutions. He believed that one of the most important effects of the 1832 Reform Bill was a 'fundamentally altered' position in terms of 'pressure and calls upon the House'. His Foreign Office circular of August 1880 asking for information on the practices of foreign legislatures for the control of debate indicated his worries. He had been impressed by the thinking of Erskine May on the problem and appeared in 1880 to prefer the devolution of work to Grand Committees to the use of clôture. May himself, however, in 1878 had hinted that he had abandoned his earlier scheme. Gladstone then commissioned J.G. Dodson to prepare memoranda on the working of the closure in the self-governing colonies as well as in foreign legislatures. At the beginning of 1881 Gladstone drafted a set of 'urgency' rules which left much of the responsibility with the Speaker. The behaviour of the Irish members over the Coercion Bill in the sitting which began on Monday 31 January and lasted for 41½ hours forced the Speaker to state that 'under the operation of the accustomed rules and methods of procedure the legislative powers of the House are paralyzed and a new and exceptional course is imperatively demanded'. The Speaker enforced 'urgency rules' but it was clear that proper reform of procedure was needed to prevent 'Parliamentary breakdown'. The autumn of 1881 saw a search for reasonable rules by Brand, May and Dodson with the purpose of repressing disorder and irregularity in the House and of easing the progress of business. The resolutions were introduced on 20 February and adopted by the end of 1882. The crucial closure division was taken on 10 November. The long fight was prolonged by what Bryce called 'the extreme conservatism of the House of Commons in all that concerns its forms'. The chief fear was that the rights of private members would suffer and that, although designed to protect governments from obstructive minorities, the new rules would strengthen the position of the large parties in the Commons. These fears were justified, but any hope that the Commons should be seen in the 1880s as a 'Grand Inquest of the Nation' rather than a working legislature was clearly unrealistic.

Thereupon Mr SPEAKER directed the Serjeant-at-Arms to remove Mr Parnell from the House.

Accordingly, the Serjeant-at-Arms, by the direction of Mr Speaker, in pursuance of the Resolution of the House, advancing to the hon. Member, invited him to retire.

Mr PARNELL: Sir, I respectfully refuse to withdraw unless I am compelled to do so by superior force.

Then the Serjeant-at-Arms (the principal Door-keeper and Messengers attending) placed his hand upon Mr Parnell, who thereupon rose and withdrew with the Serjeant-at-Arms.

Mr GLADSTONE: I think it right Sir, to take the quickest possible notice of the communication which has just been made by yourself from the Chair. You have acquainted us with the fact that, during the late division, certain hon. Members, who had challenged the judgment of the House, declined to withdraw from the House and take part in the division. That, I apprehend has been done by hon. Members who were in the House when you put the Question and when you ordered the House to be cleared. We are unaware who those hon. Members are. That is a practical objection towards taking any substantive notice of their proceedings — which, I must say, I respectfully hope will not be repeated. [*Cheers, and cries of* 'Yes; it will be!']. If that proceeding should be repeated, I respectfully hope you will support the House, and will find means of preventing a flagrant contempt of the Rules of the House and the Orders of the Chair. I will not prosecute this subject further. If the House thinks fit, I will resume my seat in order to give some other hon. Members an opportunity of expressing their opinion with regard to it. [*Cries of* 'Go on!']. I quite understand that I have hit the sentiment of the House in saying that this incident will be seriously noticed hereafter, although we are not in a condition to notice it at the present moment. I will, therefore, do my best to resume the unfortunate sentence that has been bisected and trisected. I will not inflict on the House the whole of that sentence; but I will, for a practical purpose, refer to one portion of it — that is, the closing portion of it, in which I said that the matter, which it was my heavy misfortune to approach, was a matter bristling at every point with polemical considerations and controversial matter that might become, unless great care be taken, a practical impediment to the calm and deliberate consideration of a very serious question——

Mr FINIGAN: Mr Speaker, Sir, I rise to move that the Prime Minister be no longer heard. [*Cries of* 'Order'.] I do so, Sir —— ['Chair!' *and* 'Name, Name!'].

Mr SPEAKER: I regard this as an act of wilful and deliberate obstruction, and disregard of the authority of the Chair; and I, therefore, Name you, Mr Finigan, as disregarding the authority of the Chair.

Mr FINIGAN, Member for Ennis, having been Named by Mr Speaker as disregarding the authority of the Chair ——

Motion made, and Question put, 'That Mr Finigan be suspended from the service of the House during the remainder ıof this day's sitting'. —— (*Mr Gladstone*).

The House proceeded to a Division.

Lord RICHARD GROSVENOR, one of the Tellers for the Ayes, again came to the Table and stated that he was unable to clear the House, because several Members refused to quit their places.

Mr A.M. SULLIVAN: We contest the legality of this proceeding.

Mr SPEAKER thereupon directed those Members to follow the direction of the Tellers, and he admonished them that by remaining in the House, they were resisting the authority of the Chair, and cautioned them of the consequences that their conduct might entail upon them; and then Mr SPEAKER directed that the Division should proceed.

The Tellers declared the numbers: Ayes 405; Noes 2: Majority 403——(Div. List, No.23).

NOES — Callan P., M'Kenna, Sir J.N.

TELLERS — Nolan, Major J.P., Power, R.

Mr SPEAKER thereupon directed Mr O'Donnell to withdraw.

Mr O'DONNELL: With great respect, I decline to withdraw, as a protest against Liberal Tyranny and unjust ruling.

The Serjeant-at-Arms accordingly, upon Mr Speaker's direction, removed Mr O'Donnell from the House.

Mr SPEAKER informed the House that Mr Richard Power and Mr O'Shaughnessy had been admonished by him, and cautioned for their conduct in refusing to take part in the late Division; and then Mr Speaker Named Mr Richard Power and Mr O'Shaughnessy as having disregarded the authority of the Chair.

Resolved, That Mr Richard Power and Mr O'Shaughnessy be suspended from the service of the House during the remainder of this day's sitting.—(*Mr Gladstone*).

Mr SPEAKER thereupon directed Mr Richard Power and

Mr O'Shaughnessy severally to withdraw, which direction each Member having refused to obey, the Serjeant-at-Arms, acting upon Mr Speaker's direction, removed them from the House.

Mr GLADSTONE, resuming, said: I have already said, Sir, that I dismiss from the purview of my duty on this occasion any review of the scenes that have lately taken place; but, in saying that, do not let it be supposed I, for one moment, imply that, in my opinion, they have no bearing upon the proposals to which I invite the attention of the House. On the contrary, I trust that their silent eloquence will have a large influence on the judgment of the House, and the course which it may be inclined to take with regard to the proposals of the Government. My intention is to avoid altogether epithets of praise or blame. Nothing can be more widely divergent than the opinions prevalent among the majority and the minority as to the conduct of one another, and as to the interests of which each are respectively in charge. But with these matters I do not intend to meddle in the slightest degree. They form no part of my case. My case is one that rests upon facts that are capable of being presented in the very driest form to the notice of the House. I am able to renounce, for the purposes of the present occasion, all review of the conduct of individuals; and I must endeavour to describe, in the driest terms I can command, what is the situation of the House. It will be agreed that the responsibilities of this House are measured by its powers; and as to its powers, the very first of them, I may say, in the order of nature, are its powers over its own Members for the regulation of its own proceedings. Our position, I may briefly remind the House, is altogether peculiar, and no just analogies — at all events, no sufficient analogies — can be found to apply to it from the practice of any other country in the world. There is no other country in the world in which for two or three centuries a Parliament has laboured steadily from year to year, in the face of overweening power, to build up by slow degrees a fabric of defence against that overweening power, for the purpose of maintaining and handing down intact that most precious rule of perfect liberty of speech, to which it is impossible to attach too high a price, and with respect to which we make no other demand than this — that it shall be exercised, not according to what we think reasonable, not according to what we think moderate, but simply according to the possibilities that must limit the condition and the action of a Representative Assembly. But there is another point equally vital, which it is necessary to bear in mind, if we wish to measure and gauge accurately the position of this House, as compared with other Assemblies. Other Assemblies have duties that are important, indeed; but in the mass — in the bulk — they are trifles as light as air in comparison with the duties of the British House of Commons. The British House of Commons has undertaken work with which the shoulders of human beings at any period of history and in any country in the world never have been charged. The consequence is that the very mass and amount of these duties is the measure of your weakness. Obstruction elsewhere is a jest and a plaything; Obstruction here has it in its power to place fatal, insurmountable obstacles in the way of your discharging your primary obligations. Why? Because, your duties being so many, the insufficiency of human strength, under the most favourable circumstances, places you at the mercy of those who may think fit, in the discharge of what they term their conscientious obligations, to use the Rules of debate for purposes to which they are easily capable of being applied — for the purpose of blocking the way over which you have to travel, and of rendering it impossible, within the limits of the time accorded to us as human beings, to attain to the essential matters for the transaction of which we are sent here. Liberty of speech, Sir, is not to be depreciated in anything that we say or do; but it has to be addressed to a certain end — namely the performance of public duty; and if the liberty be so used as to render the performance of that duty impossible, it must be brought within such limits — I do not say as to licence, for that we have never touched — as those who have been within this Chamber to-night may very well know — as not to debar us absolutely from fulfilling the first duties of our Parliamentary existence. And it is the first conditions of Parliamentary existence for which we are now struggling. It is not in any spirit of optimism; it is not that we may clear the road of our arrears; it is not that we may come to an ideal state, that we now propose the alteration of your Rules. It is that we may not utterly fail in that which is the very first and most elementary portion of our

task; it is that we may attain to the first condition of dignity —
nay, more, of decency; and that we may not be compelled to
render such an account of our proceedings to the country and to
our constituencies as would cover every one of us, individually
as well as collectively, with condemnation and dishonour.
What are the facts, briefly and drily stated, of the situation
before us? Sometimes it appears to be supposed, or rather taken
for granted, in Questions put in this House, that those who are
invested with the powers of government in this country from
time to time have some faculty confided to them, by the exercise
of which they can manufacture time as a manufacturer
manufactures yards of cotton. I am inclined to think at times
that if we could reverse the proceedings of a wise Pope, and
recover those 11 days that he lost for us, by obliging the
Calendar to conform to the laws of astronomy, those 11 days
might enable us to make some way with the arrears of Business.
But has the House ever considered what are the days and hours
at our command? First, let it be said that it is not a charge of
indolence that could ever be brought against the British House
of Commons. It is confessed and admitted on all hands — I do
not speak of this Parliament, but of all — that there is no
Legislative Assembly in the world that works itself so pitilessly,
so remorselessly, as the British House of Commons. If that be
so, it follows that the measure of what is done by the House is
somewhere about the utmost measure of human strength and
capacity. But let us go into the regions of possibility; let us, with
an enormous licence, imagine for a moment that it was possible
for us to devote every day in the year to the work to which we
now usually devote six or seven months; and that out of every
24 hours you could give 12 to the discharge of your
Parliamentary duties, and if you did so the calculation is a very
simple one. Deduct one-seventh for every seventh day — you
have very good reasons for deducting that seventh day, for
unless you did it, most of you would be dead before the end of
the first year — there are about 3,750 hours, which might, it is
conceivable, be used for the purposes of Parliament at all times.
And if 650 Members of this House were each of them to plead
the very moderate power of addressing the House for six hours
in the course of every Session — that is no very lengthened
period of time — six times 650 gives 3,900 hours, or 250 more

than, upon a supposition almost impossible, it could be made to yield. What is the meaning of the language that we hear about the liberties of speech? The liberties of speech! Liberty as to the quality of speech — Yes! Let none endeavour — unless under necessity, which we have never had, and are not likely to have the faintest glimmer — let none endeavour to narrow the liberal bounds that surround us in that respect. And as to the quantity of speech, it must be regulated, not by the fancies of men, but by the necessities of the case, and in accordance with the discharge of the duties which we are sent here to discharge. Our position is wholly unexampled; and I do not think I exaggerate when I say that the question of the adoption of new Rules to increase the power of the House, and to increase it effectually over those of its Members, who may be unwilling to recognize that power, is now for us a question of honour or dishonour, and in that sense — the only true sense — a question of life or death for the Parliament. How long have we been here? We have entered on the fifth week of the Session. We have had four such weeks as never opened, I believe, a Parliamentary Session in this country, for the extent and continuity of their labours. One-sixth of the whole Session gone — irrevocably gone! And what progress have we made? Our progress is this — that Her Majesty having called us together, and, in the language of Constitutional Government, having told us that a subject, in her judgment, of the utmost moment, connected with the fulfilment of the very first duties of civilized society — namely, the maintenance of peace and order in Ireland — demanded our prompt and effectual attention, the measure of the prompt and effectual attention that we have been able to give to the subject is that now in the fifth week of the Session — one-sixth of the time that will probably be at our disposal having gone — we have made just one step in the direction in which we intend to go, having passed one single initiatory stage of a Bill; and yet this has not been for want of attention or effort on the part of any Party in this House. I take this opportunity of offering to hon. Gentlemen opposite my respectful thanks, on the part of Her Majesty's Government, for the fidelity, and self-denial, and self-sacrifice with which they have come here, night after night — aye, and through night after night — to perform what they deemed to be their duty to their country. My thanks are, at least, equally due to all those whose political confidence it is our highest honour to possess, and from whom, on the present occasion, we have received the most loyal and the most enthusiastic support. But will all these efforts of all persons of authority, and of almost all private and individual Members of the House, the result is that, under a pressure of the very highest the Executive Government could put on to secure the despatch of work, the despatch which has been effected is, that before approaching one of our ordinary duties, before attempting to touch upon any special questions of the greatest importance, such as what are termed remedial measures, the vital and momentous question, for instance, of land legislation for Ireland — before we could whisper a word in the House of Commons as to the character and nature of those measures, we find ourselves entering upon the fifth week of the Session with only the sorry record of our labours to place before the world of a single stage of a single Bill, and that, necessarily, a measure of coercion, though also one of protection for Ireland, which we regard, I will not say as securing her welfare, but as securing to us the opportunity of opening a fair field from which we may legislate for her with advantage. What has been the further result of the action by which this delay has been occasioned? Private Members have been shut out from opportunities of bringing forward questions in which they take an interest; and I can assure the House that no one can feel more deeply than I the severity of the sacrifice which we have called upon them to make, and no one was more unwilling to make the claim, and accept the boon generously as it has been given. All that they have done, however, has been of avail only to secure for us that mere unit of accomplished labour to which I have referred. Eighteen nights, including one Sitting of 22 hours, and another of over 40 — [An hon. member: 41] — have been devoted entirely to a single subject, with the exception of the first night — that of the debate on the Address — which must, in any case, have been occupied by Members in the exercise of their just right of criticizing the Royal Speech and the conduct of the Government during the Recess, and another to the discussion of the affairs of the Transvaal. With those exceptions, every night has been occupied with the direct aim of reaching the result that has now been brought about, and almost invariably on the same class of topics. Two nights, indeed, were occupied with the Electoral Franchise in Ireland, and that subject was raised wholly and solely in the interest of what is called, in the scientific language of the day, the Department of Obstruction. It was not from the value attached to the Electoral Franchises in Ireland, or a claim that they were so urgent, that they required nights to be consumed in discussing them when we had an Irish Land Bill; but it was for the purpose of contributing to that aim which I now call the House to take into its firm determination to defeat. I need not dwell upon the fact that, as regards the homelier subjects of Supply and the Mutiny Act, and every other necessary matter, we have not stirred a step. Yet these, though they may not constitute the glory of Parliament, are what light and water are to a well-organized and healthy household. These conditions we have not been able to touch — conditions which we cannot longer refrain from touching, and conditions which, when we touch, the very attempt to touch will infinitely multiply the means of Obstruction, unless you, by a wise vigour, interpose, and give the securities that the case demands. Well, and by whom, let me ask, has this been done to which I have called the attention of the House? It has been done in spite of the efforts of the majority of this House. I suppose I may say, roughly, that about 500 Members of the House, of all Parties, have recorded their votes freely and repeatedly against Obstructive procedure — the proceedings which have brought us to the present pass. I will not even call them Obstructive proceedings; I will call them — I do not want to give unnecessary offence — claims of speech unlimited in the multitude of the times of its repetition, which, under the name of liberty of speech and privilege, have been an effective instrument, and have placed us in our present predicament. And what have been the forces arrayed in urging the demands which were thus made? What is the authority with which they have been pressed upon us? Have these demands been backed by the voice of the nation? There have been times when very small minorities in this House have represented the national feeling — times happily passed away never to return. Securities have been taken in the laws and institutions of the country which render such a contingency absolutely impossible. But I doubt whether any of those who have not reflected on the subject are aware how slight is the authority in comparison with that wielded by minorities in Parliament of old which can be pleaded in defence . . .

Hansard, 3rd series, cclviii, 78-9, 88-94; 3 February 1881.

31 Local Government Reform

The effect of the 1835 Municipal Corporations Act had been to set up a vast number of elected borough councils with differing functions and covering very different areas. Some aspects of their work were controlled by central government departments themselves responsible to parliament. By 1867 an immense number of local administrative units existed for such purposes as health, highways and poor relief. New school boards were added in 1870. A public health act of 1875 attempted to reduce the problem by using existing bodies as sanitary authorities. Major reform was achieved by the Municipal Corporations Act of 1882 which defined the organization and powers of municipal corporations, and by the Local Government Act of 1888 which extended the elective principle and greatly simplified the government and administrative complexity of the counties.

Constitution of County Council

1. A council shall be established in every administrative county as defined by this Act, and be entrusted with the management of the administrative and financial business of that county, and shall consist of the chairman, aldermen, and councillors.
2. The Council of a county and the members thereof shall be constituted and elected and conduct their proceedings in like manner, and be in the like position in all respects, as the council of a borough divided into wards . . .

Powers of County Council

3. There shall be transferred to the council of each county on and after the appointed day, the administrative business of the justices of the county in quarter sessions assembled, that is to say, all business done by the quarter sessions or any committee appointed by the quarter sessions, in respect of the several matters following, namely
(i)   The making, assessing, and levying of county, police,

hundred, and all rates, and the application and expenditure thereof, and the making of orders for the payment of sums payable out of any such rate or out of the county stock or county fund, and the preparation and revision of the basis or standard for the county rate:

(ii)   The borrowing of money;

(iii)   The passing of the accounts of and the discharge of the county treasurer;

(iv)   Shire halls, county halls, assize courts, judges lodgings, lock-up houses, court houses, justices rooms, police stations, and county buildings, works, and property, subject as to the use of buildings by the quarter sessions and the justices to the provisions of this Act respecting the joint committee of quarter sessions and the county council;

(v)   The licensing under any general Act of houses and other places for music or for dancing, and the granting of licences under the Racecourses Licensing Act, 1879;

(vi)   The provision, enlargement, maintenance, management, and visitation of and other dealing with asylums for pauper lunatics;

(vii)   The establishment and maintenance of and the contribution to reformatory and industrial schools;

(viii)   Bridges and roads repairable with bridges, and any powers vested by the Highways and Locomotives (Amendment) Act, 1878, in the County Authority . . .

Statutes at Large, 51 and 52 Vict., C.41.

VI

1900:
A Very Different Picture

32 Parliamentary Business

New problems were emerging by the turn of the century. In almost all areas of government they were caused by pressure of business. For Parliament even the procedural reforms of the 1880s had not provided adequate time in the session for the passing of legislation. The new closure was invoked frequently both by the government and by private members of the Commons: in the period 1897-1905 it was moved by the government 338 times and consent was refused by the Speaker only 23 times. The introduction of the 'guillotine' in 1887 to solve the weakness of the closure which could not cope with the innumerable amendments to clauses in a complex major piece of legislation had its disadvantages. The early clauses of a bill could be fully discussed whereas no debate would be permitted on the later ones. This problem was largely remedied with the Home Rule Bill of 1893: a resolution laid out a timetable for different clauses. This type of closure by compartment was used for the Evicted Tenants Bill of 1894 and the Education Bill of 1902, that is where the House agreed the bills under consideration were difficult. This procedure was not mentioned in the Standing Orders.

After 1896 private members were reduced to narrow confines, being limited to Tuesdays in the middle of the Session and Wednesday afternoons up to the fortnight after Whitsuntide. Their real gain had however been the increasingly permitted use of the parliamentary question. By the 1890s the number of questions on the notice papers for one Session could be as high as 5,000. By 1900 the supplementary or subsidiary question had become accepted. Since private members could normally no longer use the adjournment motion to raise urgent problems, it would have seemed unreasonable for the government to resist the emergence of the supplementary question. Great delays were being caused by the increasing number of questions and opposed private business. The equivalent of four parliamentary days a year was spent on opposed private business in the

175

period 1896 to 1900. Public business often did not start till 6 p.m. each day. Few significant speeches by leading members were made between 7 and 10 p.m. since it was generally assumed that most members were at dinner. The bitterly fought session of 1901 brought matters to a head and, after much haggling, a number of fundamental reforms were instituted in 1902, largely on the initiative of Balfour. These came to be called the 'Parliamentary Railway Timetable'. Government business was given precedence for almost all the session. The House was to sit early in the afternoon: questions were given a time limit of half an hour in which only those questions for which members specifically demanded an oral answer were taken. A distinction was therefore drawn between a question needing a factual answer which could be given in Hansard *and one asked for political reasons. There were to be two sittings on most days to give a break for dinner: these two sittings were run together after 1906.*

The improvements in the facilities for government business derived however as much from the refinement of the two-party system and greater self-discipline on the part of the major parties as they did from further reforms in parliamentary procedure. The changes in the period 1830 to 1906 had seen a fundamental reshaping of the Commons to fit its legislative purpose. The House of 1910 may have been composed of very much the same men as that of 1800 in terms of professional and social background, but it functioned in a completely different manner.

(a) A.J. BALFOUR

Leader of the Conservative and Unionist Party in the Commons

Let me just ask the House — and this will conclude my preliminary statement — to compare, in three features, the years 1800 and 1901. In 1800 the House sat on portions of 72 days. Unfortunately the records of *Hansard* do not enable us to tell how long the sittings were. In 1901 the House sat 115 days and these sittings, as hon. Gentlemen know to their cost, were in many cases extremely prolonged. In 1800 Supply took one day; in 1901 it took 26 days. In 1800 not a single Question was put during the whole course of Parliament. In 1901, including Supplementary Questions, it has been calculated for me that 7,180 Questions were asked. These 7,180 Questions occupied 119 hours; in other words, they occupied close upon 15 eight-hour Parliamentary days, or three weeks of Government time. Finally, though this is of less importance, the Address in

1800, and for very many years after that, down to my own memory, was voted in one day. Last year it could only be voted in nine. The truth is that, with the changing circumstances of the House, in itself revolutionary, our rules, which were originally framed as it were to promote a fertilising and irrigating flow of eloquence, are now, it appears, required to dam up its vast and destructive floods, and keep them within reasonable limits.

May I conclude, Sir, by deprecating criticism from two quarters, I hope that nobody will criticise that part of our scheme which is intended to meet the convenience of Members, who does not himself suffer from the inconvenience which Members who attend are now suffering from. I hope, for example, that no man will sneer at our arrangement for a dinner hour unless he can show to the satisfaction of the House that he has dined here at least once a week during his Parliamentary career. I hope, in the second place, that no man will meet us by saying that we are abandoning the old traditions of this House and throwing away safeguards which were once found necessary in our constitution. After all, Charles I is not knocking at our door now, and our business is not to fight with the Crown. The dangers that we have to fear are not the dangers which our ancestors had to fear; and the fact that we put our bows and arrows in a museum does not at all show that we are insensible of the real practical necessities of the age. Let us endeavour to face the facts of Parliamentary life as we find them. Let every man sitting on this side of the House contemplate these rules as if he were tomorrow going to sit on the other side of the House. And, *per contra*, let every Gentleman on the opposite side of the House remember that the time may come when he may sit on this side . . . I do not know whether my appeal has fallen short of hon. Members below the gangway; but at any rate it has its significance with regard to Gentlemen sitting in all other parts of the House. We do not pretend that this is a complete scheme or a final scheme; and we do not believe in finality in these matters. But we do believe that these reforms will add enormously to the convenience of the House, and shorten some unnecessary opportunities for debate, and that they will yet leave this House what it always has been and ought to be — not merely a machine for passing legislation, but a free arena in which questions interesting to the country may be freely discussed.

Hansard, 4th series, ci, 1352-3, 1373; 30 January 1902.

(b) SIR HENRY CAMPBELL-BANNERMAN

Leader of the Liberal Party in the Commons

Now let us look at the present proposals. Do they justify careful and deliberate examination by the House? Why, Sir, there have not, within your recollection, been proposals laid before this House so grave, so extensive, so far-reaching, so heterogenous, interfering as they do, with the almost immemorial arrangements, in some particulars, of this House in the matter of time; and also treading very seriously on the immemorial rights of the House.

Now, Sir, when we speak of rights of the House, and the rights of private Members, I think that sometimes we have a little confusion in our minds; there is the right of private Members who have introduced Bills of their own, or who wish to bring before the House Motions of their own. I admit, for my part, that that is not now so important a function of the private Member as it was some twenty or thirty or forty years ago. With regard to the Motions, the development of the Press and the activity of the Press in all directions, the multiplication of magazines and other publications of that kind have taken away the necessity that then existed for an ample opportunity to private Members to introduce Motions for merely educative purposes, in order to instruct and inform the opinion of the House and of the public. I fully admit that something has occurred in that direction. I admit also that such is the pressure of business in the House that the private Members have less and less chances of effective legislation; and the power to legislate falls more and more into the hands of the Government of the day. I admit all this, but there is something quite apart from this right of the private Member to move and to introduce a Bill on his own account; there is the general right of the House to interrogate Ministers and discuss questions, and to inform

178

the opinion of the country by so doing. It is a diffused right in which we all take a share, and in the duty of exercising which we must all take our part. And it is this, I think, which is the most important thing to bear in mind when we speak of the rights of the House and the rights of private Members.

After all, Sir, there is an old phrase, which may sound a mere rhetorical form of words, that this House is 'the grand inquest of the nation'; but that really does express the foundation truth of the duty of the House of Commons. This is not a mere factory of statutes; not a mere counting-house, in which demands on the public purse are being checked, approved, and provided for; it is something much more, and much more important. For my part I would go so far as to say, that efficiency in the conduct of business is merely secondary to the maintenance of those rights of which I speak; and it would be better that the House should be less efficient in its transactions of business, and retain the full faculty of exercising the functions to which I refer, rather than that it should be diminished, and the House should become the most perfect legislative machine in the world. Therefore, the conclusion we are brought to by these considerations is surely this — that this matter is not the affair of the Government, it is not the affair of the majority, it is not the affair of any section large or small of the House. It is the affair of the House itself. And that, I think, points as directly as anything can point to the reference of such a matter as this, so complicated, so grave, so far-reaching in its consequences, to a Select Committee, where the House of Commons could be fortified by the opinion and the judgment of its most important Members.

Well, I need hardly say, having just expressed what my view of the subject-matter with which we have to deal is, that there is no room here for Party spirit. We do not look on this question in the least degree from that point of view, at least that I can honestly say for myself. We are indebted to the Government for having embodied in these proposed alterations their view, their experience, from their own standpoint, of what is required; but let it not be forgotten that they put those proposals forward not as their own plan designed for their own purposes. They put them forward avowedly as the mouthpiece of the House. It appears to me, in looking at this large and important question, there are one or two considerations that we ought to keep steadily in view. First of all, we ought to make sure that the state of things which we desire to meet by alterations in our Rules is a permanent and not an accidental and transitory state of things. The Rules should not be designed to meet circumstances which may not continue for any length of time. They must not be based, for instance, on a consideration of the present distribution of Members of the House. That may last, it may become more — if I may use the word — lop-sided than at present, it may become less so. None of us have the gift of prophecy; we cannot say. All we can say is that theHouse as at present constituted, as between Parties, is not in a normal condition, and therefore, anything we may do with a view to meet the particular exigencies of the present situation may not be a proper course for us to take in view of the ordinary and normal state of things.

Then again, I would say that we should go very far wrong if we passed rules which were aimed at any particular section of the House which was supposed to be somewhat out of harmony with the majority of the House. I may imagine a case in which a certain section of Members rather wished to be considered to be out of harmony with the majority of the House. But we should not found our rules on that supposition, for surely we may hope that that also is a transitory state of things.

The next view I would urge is one which, on first night of the session I ventured to express in a very few words — that we ought not to be governed too much by the consideration of the mere personal convenience and comfort of the Members . . . Then the third point I would venture to bring before the House is this — which also I mentioned on a previous occasion — that we must take care that we do not, wittingly or unwittingly, exalt the power of the Executive and diminish the control of the House at large. Facilitate the progress of business as much as you like, make it as reasonable and as easy as you like; but do not do anything which will have the effect of placing the House of Commons more and more at the mercy of the Government of the day.

Hansard, 4th series, cii, 549-552; 6 February 1902.

(c) JOSEPH CHAMBERLAIN

Joseph Chamberlain was Colonial Secretary 1895-1903, under Lord Salisbury's premiership.

Any change ought to be based on an endeavour to meet the convenience of the whole House. If it is impossible to do that, if you cannot secure convenience for some without inconvenience for others, then the principle should be to secure the convenience of the majority, and of course the vote of the House, after the discussion, will show on which side the convenience of the majority lies. I do not think it at all probable that the convenience of any small section of the House, or any exceptional demand is at all likely to weigh with the House. The last principle laid down by the right hon. Gentleman was that we ought not to exalt the Executive at the cost of the whole House. I often hear some learned and right hon. Gentlemen on both sides of the House endeavour to distinguish between the Government and the House, between the Executive and the House. After all, the Government are the servants of the House. They are chosen practically with the approval of the House. Of course, when we speak of the House, we always mean the majority of the House — the majority for the time being. The approval of the House is the breath of our existence. We can be turned out of office tomorrow or tonight by a simple change of opinion which would cause us to be out of sympathy with the majority of the House. Therefore, when you talk about curtailing the powers of the Government, what you mean, and it is better to say so at once, is curtailing the powers of the majority, and increasing the powers of the minority. ['No, no.'] I have placed my reason for thinking so before you, and my belief is that that is the inevitable result of the line of argument. If it be so I can give to it no support whatever. I believe that the people who elect the majority of the House have a right to see that that majority has power to carry out what is *ex hypothesi* the will of the majority of the nation; and our elections and our representative system are a perfect and absolute farce if with one hand you pretend that the majority elects a Government, and then with the other hand prevent that Government from doing its proper work. With these qualifications I say that I see no objection to the principles which the right hon. Gentleman laid down, and upon which I have no doubt the House generally will agree.

I cannot go back as far as the right hon. Gentleman, but I can go back twenty-six years; and I say that the situation in the House of Commons then was totally different. It was not made by Rules, it is true. It was made to a great extent by the courtesy which all sections at that time were ready to show one to another. At that time no man would have dared to set himself against what may be called the general feeling of the House; and that desire to earn the good opinion of the House as a whole did act as a great restriction upon anything in the nature of undesirable prolixity. But that is not all. What were the customs of the House at that time? We came down a little later than now, and then we had Questions. But how many? Not a third of the average number of questions for last session. And the cross-questioning of Ministers which now goes on in the form of supplementary questions was practically unknown. Hardly ever was a second question asked. A Member, having put his Question, was satisfied with the answer which the Minister gave, and no attempt was made to extract by some sudden question information which perhaps it might not be in the public interest for the Minister to give. We always knew then what we were coming down for; and the order of debate was generally such that it was perfectly possible for a man, having attended the first hour or two of the sitting, to know whether he would be wanted again that night, and if so, when he would be wanted. There was always an understanding between the two sides as to when a division would be taken. But note what that means. See how it contributed to the convenience of Members on both sides of the House. It was quite possible for a man to go away — and many did go away — for dinner. Is it to be represented as a crime that a Member who is, according to the condition of the right hon. Gentleman, resident in London, should prefer on the whole, much as he likes the House of Commons, to spend if he can an hour or two with his family, and to spend that time at dinner, or that he should prefer, if he has no family, to dine with his friends?

Hansard, 4th series, cii, 567-8, 574; 6 February 1902.

(d) JAMES BRYCE

Bryce, historian and jurist, was a Liberal member of Parliament

Let me say at once that I think there is a very strong case for change. I am not one of those who believe that our present Rules are perfect and do not require alteration. There is hardly a branch of our Standing Orders in which some improvement might not be made. I am glad, therefore, that the matter has been taken up, but it has been taken up in a very imperfect way. There are many points, some of them quite as important as those with which the Government propose to deal, passed over in silence. There is the question of the substitution of some system of choice for the system of chance by which the Motions and Bills of private Members are brought before the House. The present system involves constant waste of time on matters about which nobody cares, and gives us year after year a group of insignificant measures which take up time that otherwise might be devoted to the consideration of questions of importance. As far back as 1887, I brought forward a suggestion on this subject, which had the support of many Members of weight, and I regret the Government have not taken the matter in hand, as it is very important.

Now I come to a question of private Members. There is a tendency to disparage private Members' legislation. Many Members think it is unimportant. That is a new thing in the House. When I entered Parliament in 1880 many of the best and most useful Bills passed by the House, were introduced by private Members. They were not Bills which excited political conflict, out of which party capital could be made, but they dealt with comparatively small defects in the law, which the Government did not care to deal with, but of which the private Member happened to know, and thus they were remedied. In those days a private Member could hope to carry his Bill; there were opportunities of doing so. I have known a good many Bills to get their Second Reading on a Wednesday, and then be dealt with in Committee in useful and practical debate between twelve and two o'clock in the morning, when nobody stayed except those interested. It is a great loss to the country that private Members can no longer pass such Bills, and it is a great pity to lose the opportunity which these rules afford of endeavouring to restore to some extent the private Member's chance of passing such legislation. People say, 'Oh, but private Members waste so much of their time on frivolous Bills.' Why is that? Because of the ballot. The House has no means by which it can make any useful choice between frivolous and important Bills. For that reason Bills come up year after year — and occupy a good deal of time — which ought to be dealt with once and for all.

The British Constitution requires that the House of Commons should give constant criticism, and if the theory of the Colonial Secretary were correct it would be sufficient if the House met once a month and gave a vote of confidence in the Government, and allowed them to go on. That is the danger of the doctrine of the Colonial Secretary, who said that he meant a majority of the House when he spoke of the House. The House does not mean a majority but the House as a whole, because as we perfectly well know, the tendency of a majority always is to accelerate business and to give support to the Government for that purpose. Therefore it is necessary that the House should be recognised for the sake of the country which is more likely to find a voice through the minority than it will through the majority.

What I complain of is the loss of what my right hon. friend calls the diffused control of the House, and it is the loss of this constant criticism and oversight by these changes in our Rules which many of us fear: and I am bound to say in regard to the Rules as a whole, that although I see many points in which they contain valuable truths, I do think that there is a tendency to bring about a certain loss of interest on the part of a large number of hon. Members in the business of the House. Even now there are amongst hon. Members those who will tell you privately that they are disappointed with the House because they find that there is so little that a private member can do. I have known them very disappointed at finding how little they can make use of their attainments and I have known men of great ability give up Parliamentary work because they have found that, after a few years in the House, they were spending their time to little or no purpose. That is one of the things which we ought to endeavour to avert, and we ought to make the House attractive to that class of men. When I look at the Rules as a whole, I am inclined to fear that the tendency will be for a large number of hon. Members to pay less attention to the business of the House except when some keen political controversy is going on. I am afraid that at other times the attendance will be more scanty. And yet, is it not in these times of warm political controversy that the best work of Parliament is done? If the interest of hon. Members is slackened by making the House more agreeable to our easy-going hon. Members, a more copious legislative output will be no compensation for rendering the House less attractive to those diligent and public-spirited of the Members, for even although our legislation may be more and passed more promptly, we shall have attained little by these Rules, and the labour we are now spending upon them will have been spent in vain.

Hansard, 4th series, cii, 763-772; 7 February 1902.

33 Delegated Legislation

Probably the growth of delegated legislation and the ever extending use of administrative discretion were the best indicators of government activity in the late nineteenth century. During the century the practice of passing legislation of a general kind was accepted by Parliament, who became more and more willing to leave the administration with general authority to act both executively and legislatively. The shortage of parliamentary time and the increasing complexity of legislation encouraged the use of delegation. The amount of delegation varied. In 1860, 33 out of 154 statutes delegated some powers while in 1880 only 7 out of 48 Acts did so. The practice and range of delegated legislation, however, tended to grow. From 1890 the Statutory Rules and Orders were published: between 1894 and 1900 the average annual number of Orders made was about 1,000 and by 1914 was over 1,300. Departments varied in their reliance on delegation and in the kind of powers taken. Constitutional authorities tended to approve these changes. The Rules Publication Act of 1893 provided that statutory rules and orders must be published in the London

Gazette *forty days before coming into operation, thereby allowing interested parties an opportunity to object to them. At the time, Sir Henry Jenkyns, a Parliamentary counsel, considered such statutory rules to be 'of great public advantage, because the details which are the subject of them can thus be regulated after a Bill passes into an Act with greater care and minuteness, and with better adaptation to local or other special circumstances, than they possibly can be in the passage of a Bill through Parliament'. Maitland (33a) realized that the increased use of delegation represented a 'new departure' for the British Constitution. Dicey (33b) misunderstood French administrative law in his comparative comments, and Sir Courtenay Ilbert (33c), seemed quite happy with the trend.*

(a) F.W. MAITLAND

These extracts are taken from lectures given in 1887 and 1888

This is the result of a modern movement, a movement which began, we may say, about the time of the Reform Bill of 1832. The new wants of a new age have been met in a new manner — by giving statutory powers of all kinds, sometimes to the Queen in Council, sometimes to the Treasury, sometimes to a Secretary of State, sometimes to this Board, sometimes to the other. But of this vast change our institutional writers have hardly yet taken into account. They go on writing as though England were governed by the royal prerogatives, as if ministers had nothing else to do than to advise the king as to how his prerogatives should be exercised.

In my view, which I put forward with some diffidence and with a full warning that it is not orthodox, we no longer say that the executive power is vested in the king: the king has powers, this minister has powers, and that minister has powers. The requisite harmony is secured by the extra-legal organization of cabinet and ministry. The powers legally given to the king, are certainly the most important, but I cannot consent to call them supreme. To be able to declare war and peace is certainly an important power, perhaps the most important power that the law can give, and this belongs to the king. But the power to make rules for the government of the police force is also an important power, and this our law gives to a secretary of state. The one power may be vastly more important than the other, but it is in no sense supreme over the other. The supremacy of the king's powers, if it is to be found anywhere, must be found in the fact, that the ministers legally hold their offices during his good pleasure.

. . . I say of constitutional law, for it seems to me impossible so to define constitutional law that it shall not include the constitution of every organ of government whether it be central or local, whether it be sovereign or subordinate. It must deal not only with the king, the parliament, the privy council, but also with the justices of the peace, the guardians of the poor, the Boards of Health, the School Boards, and again with the constitution of the Treasury, of the Education Department, of the Courts of Law. Naturally it is with the more exalted parts of the subject that we are chiefly concerned; they are the more intelligible and the more elementary: but we must not take a part for the whole or suppose that matters are unimportant because we have not yet had time to explore them thoroughly. Year by year the subordinate government of England is becoming more and more important. The new movement set in with the Reform Bill of 1832: it has gone far already and assuredly it will go further. We are becoming a much governed nation, governed by all manner of councils and boards and officers, central and local, high and low, exercising the powers which have been committed to them by modern statutes.

Constitutional History of England (Cambridge, 1909), pp. 417-18, 500-1.

(b) A.V. DICEY

Dicey led his readers to believe that French administrative law placed officials in a specially privileged position rather than gave the subject considerable protection against illegal state action. So convinced was he of the strengths and virtues of the English rule of law that he appeared to accept the ever-expanding executive powers as aids to strong government without realizing how far they encroached on the principles he admired.

It is, however, this very contrast between administrative law as it exists in France, and still more as it existed during by far the greater part of the nineteenth century, and the notions of equality before the law of the land which are firmly established in modern England, that mainly makes it worth while to study, not of course the details, but what Tocqueville calls the *notions générales* of French *droit administratif*. Our aim should be to seize the general nature of administrative law and the principles on which the whole system of *droit administratif* depends, to note the salient characteristics by which this system is marked, and, lastly, to make clear to ourselves how it is that the existence of a scheme of administrative law makes the legal situation of every government official in France different from the legal situation of servants of the State in England, and in fact establishes a condition of things fundamentally inconsistent with what Englishmen regard as the due supremacy of the ordinary law of the land.

Anyone who considers with care the nature of the *droit administratif* of France, or the topics to which it applies, will soon discover that it rests, and always has rested, at bottom on two leading ideas alien to the conceptions of modern Englishmen.

The first of these ideas is that the government, and every servant of the government, possesses, as representative of the nation, a whole body of special rights, privileges, or prerogatives as against private citizens, and that the extent of these rights, privileges, or prerogatives is to be determined on principles different from the considerations which fix the legal rights and duties of one citizen towards another. An individual in his dealings with the State does not, according to French ideas, stand on anything like the same footing as that on which he stands in dealings with his neighbour . . .

. . . The fourth and most despotic characteristic of *droit administratif* lies in its tendency to protect from the supervision or control of the ordinary law Courts any servant of the State who is guilty of an act, however illegal, whilst acting in *bona fide* obedience to the orders of his superiors and, as far as intention goes, in the mere discharge of his official duties.

An intelligent student soon finds that *droit administratif* contains rules as to the status, the privileges, and the duties of government officials. He therefore thinks he can identify it with the laws, regulations, or customs which in England determine the position of the servants of the Crown, or (leaving the army out of consideration) of the Civil Service. Such 'official law' exists, though only to a limited extent, in England no less than in France, and it is of course possible to identify and compare this official law of the one country with the official law of the other. But further investigation shows that official law thus understood, though it may form part of, is a very different thing from *droit administratif*. The law, by whatever name we term it, which regulates the privileges or disabilities of civil servants is the law of a class, just as military law is the law of a class, namely, the army. But *droit administratif* is not the law of a class, but — a very different thing — a body of law which, under given circumstances, may affect the rights of any French citizen, as for example, where an action is brought by A against X in the ordinary Courts (*tribunaux judiciaires*), and the rights of the parties are found to depend on an administrative act (*acte administratif*), which must be interpreted by an administrative tribunal (*tribunal administratif*). In truth, *droit administratif* is not the law of the Civil Service, but is that part of French public law which affects every Frenchman in relation to the acts of the public administration as the representative of the State. The relation indeed of *droit administratif* to the ordinary law of France may be best compared not with the relation of the law governing a particular class (e.g. military law) to the general law of England, but with the relation of Equity to the common law of England. The point of likeness, slight though in other respects it be, is that *droit administratif* in France and Equity in England each constitute a body of law which differs from the ordinary law of the land, and under certain circumstances modifies the ordinary civil rights of every citizen.

When our student finds that *droit administratif* cannot be identified with the law of the Civil Service, he naturally enough imagines that it may be treated as the sum of all the laws which confer special powers and impose special duties upon the administration, or, in other words, which regulate the functions of the Government. Such laws, though they must exist in every country, have till recently been few in England, simply because in England the sphere of the State's activity has, till within the last fifty or sixty years, been extremely limited. But even in England laws imposing special functions upon government officials have always existed, and the number thereof has of late vastly increased; to take one example among a score, the Factory legislation, which has grown up mainly during the latter half of the nineteenth century, has, with regard to the inspection and regulation of manufactories and workshops, given to the Government and its officials wide rights, and imposed upon them wide duties. If, then, *droit administratif* meant nothing more than the sum of all the laws which determine the functions of civil servants, *droit administratif* might be identified in its general character with the governmental law of England. The idea that such an identification is possible is encouraged by the wide definitions of *droit administratif* to be gathered from French works of authority, and by the vagueness with which English writers occasionally use the term 'administrative law'. But here, again, the attempted identification breaks down. *Droit administratif*, as it exists in France, is not the sum of the powers possessed or of the functions discharged by the administration; it is rather the sum of the principles which govern the relation between French citizens, as individuals, and the administration as the representative of the State. Here we touch upon the fundamental difference between English and French ideas. In England the powers of the Crown and its servants may from time to time be increased as they may also be diminished. But these powers, whatever they are, must be exercised in accordance with the ordinary common law principles which govern the relation of one Englishman to another. A factory inspector, for example, is possessed of peculiar powers conferred upon him by Act of Parliament; but if in virtue of the orders of his superior officials he exceeds the authority given him by law, he becomes at once responsible for the wrong done, and cannot plead in his defence strict obedience to official orders, and, further, for the tort he has committed he becomes amenable to the ordinary Courts. In France, on the other hand, whilst the powers placed in the hands of the administration might be diminished, it is always assumed that the relation of individual citizens to the State is regulated by principles different from those which govern the relation of one French citizen to another. *Droit administratif*, in short, rests upon ideas absolutely foreign to English law: the one, as I have already explained, is that the relation of individuals to the State is governed by principles essentially different from those rules of private law which govern the rights of private persons towards their neighbours; the other is that questions as to the application of these principles do not lie within the jurisdiction of the ordinary Courts. This essential difference renders the identification of *droit administratif* with any branch of English law an impossibility. Hence inquiries which rightly occupy French jurists, such, for example, as what is the proper definition of the *contentieux administratif*; what is the precise difference between *actes de gestion* and *actes de puissance publique*, and generally, what are the boundaries between the jurisdiction of the ordinary Courts (*tribunaux judiciaires*) and the jurisdiction of the administrative Courts (*tribunaux administratifs*) have under English law no meaning.

Has *droit administratif* been of recent years introduced in any sense into the law of England?

This is an inquiry which has been raised by writers of eminence, and which has caused some perplexity. We may give thereto a decided and negative reply.

The powers of the English Government have, during the last sixty years or so, been largely increased; the State has undertaken many new functions, such, for example, as the regulation of labour under the Factory Acts, and the supervision of public education under the Education Acts. Nor is the importance of this extension of the activity of the State lessened by the consideration that its powers are in many cases exercised by local bodies, such, for example, as County Councils. But though the powers conferred on persons or bodies who directly or indirectly represent the State have been greatly increased in many directions, there has been no intentional introduction into the law of England of the essential principles of *droit administratif*. Any official who exceeds the authority given him by the law incurs the common law responsibility for his wrongful act; he is amenable to the authority of the ordinary Courts, and the ordinary Courts have themselves jurisdiction to determine what is the extent of his legal power, and whether the orders under which he has acted were legal and valid. Hence the Courts do in effect limit and interfere with the action of the 'administration', using that word in its widest sense. The London School Board, for example, has claimed and exercised the right to tax the ratepayers for the support of a kind of education superior to the elementary teaching generally provided by School Boards; the High Court of Justice has decided that such right does not exist. A year or two ago some officials, acting under the distinct orders of the Lords of the Admiralty, occupied some land alleged to belong to the Crown; the title of the Crown being disputed, a court of law gave judgment against the officials as wrong-doers. In each of these cases nice and disputable points of law were raised, but no English lawyer, whatever his opinion of the judgments given by the Court, has ever doubted that the High Court had jurisdiction to determine what were the rights of the School Board or of the Crown.

Droit administratif, therefore, has obtained no foothold in England, but, as has been pointed out by some foreign critics, recent legislation has occasionally, and for particular purposes, given to officials something like judicial authority. It is possible in such instances, which are rare, to see a slight approximation to *droit administratif*, but the innovations, such as they are, have been suggested merely by considerations of practical convenience, and do not betray the least intention on the part of English statesmen to modify the essential principles of English law. There exists in England no true *droit administratif*.

Law of the Constitution (1885; cited from 8th edition, Macmillan, 1931), pp. 327-8, 332, 341, 380-6.

(c) SIR COURTENAY ILBERT

Parliamentary counsel to the Treasury

On the other hand, the increasing complexity of modern administration, and the increasing difficulty of passing complicated measures through the ordeal of parliamentary discussion, has led to an increase in the practice of delegating legislative powers to executive authorities . . .

. . . The tendency of modern parliamentary legislation in England has been in the direction of placing in the body of an

Act merely a few broad general rules or statements of principles, and relegating details either to schedules or to statutory rules.

The shifting of the centre of political gravity after the Reform Act of 1832, the enormous strides of scientific discovery, commercial enterprise, and industrial activity, the new problems presented by the massing of great numbers in towns and factories under artificial conditions, the awakened interest in the moral, mental, and material welfare of the working classes, involving demands for enlargement of the functions both of the central and of the local government — all these causes have materially altered the character and increased the volume of Victorian legislation. New authorities have been created with new duties, new powers, and new areas. And care has not always been taken to fit the new system into the old, or to harmonize with each other the functions of co-existing authorities. Hence the chaos of rates, areas, and authorities with which we are all familiar and which has not been abolished, though it has been to some extent reduced, by recent local government legislation.

The net result of the legislative activity which has characterized, though with different degrees of intensity, the period since 1832, has been the building up piecemeal of an administrative machine of great complexity, which stands in as constant need of repair, renewal, reconstruction, and adaptation to new requirements as the plant of a modern factory. The legislation required for this purpose is enough, and more than enough, to absorb the whole legislative time of the House of Commons, and the problem of finding the requisite time for this class of legislation increases in difficulty every year, and taxes to the utmost, if it does not baffle, the ingenuity of those who are responsible for the arrangement of parliamentary business.

Rightly or wrongly, Englishmen have an instinctive distrust of official discretion, an instinctive scepticism about bureaucratic wisdom, and they have carried this feeling with them into the

United States and the British Colonies. They are ready enough, they are often embarrassingly eager to confer new powers on the executive authority, central or local. But they like to determine for themselves how those powers are to be exercised. They like to see, in black and white, the rules by which their liberty of action is restrained and to have an effective share in the making of those rules. And they insist on the meaning of those rules being determined, not by administrative authorities, nor by any special tribunal, but by the ordinary law courts of the country. This is the peculiarity which constitutes the most marked distinction between British and American legislation on the one hand, and Continental legislation on the ·other, and which makes the framework and arrangement of an English statute such an incomprehensible puzzle to the ordinary Continental student of laws.

It is quite true that English legislation has recently shown a tendency to assimilate to Continental methods, not indeed in the reference to exceptional tribunals of questions as to the meaning of legislative enactments, but in the avoidance of unnecessary details. The modern English statute is couched in more general terms, descends less into minute details, and leaves a wider range for subordinate legislation and a wider scope for official discretion in the execution and development of the law, than its predecessor of forty or fifty years ago. This tendency makes for perspicuity as well as brevity, and therefore for improvement in the form of the law. But it must not be exaggerated or abused. The instinctive English distrust of official discretion and jealousy of encroachments by the executive on the sphere of the legislature, still exists, and unless the temper of Parliament should materially change, will continue to exist, and to be an important factor in the form of Parliamentary legislation. If any minister doubts their existence, let him yield to the temptation of asking for power to exercise departmental discretion, or to make departmental rules, in terms wider and more unrestricted than the circumstances of the case may require. He is pretty sure to receive from his own side hints, friendly but unmistakable, that powers of this kind can only be obtained by general consent, and that if opposition is threatened from any quarter, he will do well to draw in his horns and be more modest in his drafts on the confidence of the House. Opposition may often be averted by prudent limitation of the powers asked for, either by specifying more minutely the purposes for which they are to be exercised, or by submitting their exercise to the approval of Parliament. And care should be taken that the control thus reserved is real and not illusory. The practice under which schemes and rules requiring Parliamentary approval are brought on for discussion after midnight makes Parliament more reluctant than it would otherwise be to concede to the executive the power of making such schemes and rules. And finally, it must be remembered that Parliament, whilst casting on the executive the responsibility for the initiation and framing of its more important legislative measures, and delegating to the executive, under due limitations, the power of supplementing these measures by subordinate rules, yet jealously reserves to the ordinary courts of the country the exclusive right and power of interpreting all enactments, whether made directly by Parliament, or under powers delegated to an executive authority. Therefore, not only Acts of Parliament, but rules made under statutory powers, ought to be expressed with such technical accuracy and precision as will enable them to face the ordeal of judicial interpretation.

Legislative Methods and Forms (Oxford, 1901), pp. 37, 212-13, 220-2.

34 Government Finance and Taxation

Although, as Henry Roseveare has shown in The Treasury, *the level of central and local government spending remained relatively steady throughout the nineteenth century, defence and social expenditure gradually came to take a more significant share of the total. The growing costs of services such as education and the factory inspectorate were becoming major items of national expenditure. The controlling position of the Treasury and the tradition of seeking economy for its own sake were, in 1900, coming under attack within the Cabinet, Parliament and the country. Harcourt's new death duty introduced in 1894 the principle of taxation graduated in relation to the ability to pay. The concept of the income tax as an emergency measure had become anachronistic.*

(a) THE COST OF EDUCATION

. . . £803,794 was voted in 1861-62, and £842,119 in 1862-63. The latter year marks an epoch in the history of the Estimate, because it was in July 1862 that the Revised Code of 1862 came into force in England and Wales. The Estimate for 1863-64 amounted to £804,002 of which £316,221 was payable under the code of 1860; this year was therefore one of transition, and the details of the Estimate exhibited both the old and the new systems. The Estimate for 1864-65 amounted to £705,404; it exhibited the new system in complete working, except as regards Scotland. The main feature of the change was the substitution, for the former complicated system of payments, of annual grants to Elementary Schools, dependent mainly on the results of the examination and the attendance of scholars; and it will be observed that more stringent inspection led to a decrease in the amount payable from the Vote. The amount voted in 1865-66 was £693,078, for 1866-67, £694,530, for 1867-68, £705,865, for 1868-69, £781,324; the grants in all these years being based, for England, on the Code of 1862 (revised from time to time), and for Scotland on that of 1860, as regards grants, although the inspection was conducted under the later Code. In 1868-69 the Estimate was first divided into sub-heads in accordance with the practice then introduced generally under the Exchequer and Audit Act. The Estimate, as originally presented in that year, amounted to £842,554, being based on the assumption that the Education Bill of that Session would become law; but a revised estimate was substituted when that Bill was withdrawn. In 1869-70, £840,711 was voted on the same system as before, and £914,721 in 1870-71. In 1871-72, however, the system of grants was revolutionised, as regards England, by the New Code of 1871, issued under the Elementary Education Act of 1870; the Estimate increased by £543,681 to £1,458,402, including £70,000 for 'Organization of Districts' under the new Act. In 1872-73, it amounted to £1,551,560. In 1873-74 the provision for Scottish Education (except salaries at headquarters) was formed into a separate estimate, the subsequent history of which belongs to the Note upon that Vote; the estimate for England and Wales amounted to £1,299,603, a decrease of £101,952 on the corresponding figure for the previous year. After that year there was a steady increase, the Votes having been, for 1874-75, £1,356,852; 1875-76, £1,548,563; 1876-77, £1,707,055; 1877-78, £1,910,829; 1878-89, £2,149,208; 1879-80, £2,481,168; 1880-81, £2,536,077; 1881-82, £2,683,958; 1882-83, £2,791,985; 1883-84, £2,938,930; 1884-85, £3,180,572; 1885-86, £3,302,772; 1886-87, £3,422,989; 1887-88, £3,458,807; and 1888-89, £3,600,767.

Treasury Papers, Public Record Office, T.165/24 Board of Education, p.2.

(b) LORD SALISBURY: CRITICISM OF TREASURY CONTROL

Lord Salisbury was speaking as Prime Minister in the debate on the Queen's Speech and commenting on criticism of the government's conduct of the war in South Africa.

. . . But the moral I wish to draw from this uniformity of experience is that it is not the extraordinary folly or feebleness of particular Ministers or generals with which you have to deal, which is the sole cause of your reverses. There must be something else. We cannot have been so unlucky as to have fought four times and to have lighted upon the most incompetent and worthless Ministers that the world has ever produced. It is evident there is something in your machinery that is wrong . . . Of course, first and foremost stands conscription, and no one imagines, even among the youngest of us, that he will ever live to see conscription adopted in this country. Then comes the employment as experts of persons sitting in Parliament exercising power over the military administration, who are named by the Government, but who have not to obtain the approval of the electors and the constituencies. It is an important and very difficult question. Then there is the big question of promotion by seniority, a delicate subject; but I doubt if you will find that promotion by seniority prevails in any of the great armies of Europe to the extent it prevails here. Then there is that matter of secret service to which I have already referred. There is no other country which is content to protect itself with so slight a supply of funds as our own; and last of all I feel I am laying my hand on the sacred feature of the Constitution when I say there is the Treasury. At the present time I feel assured that the powers of the Treasury have been administered with the greatest judgment, and the greatest consideration, and do not imagine for a moment that I support the idiotic attacks which have been made on the present Chancellor of the Exechequer. He is a Minister who has filled the office with the greatest consideration to the powers of the Treasury; but I say that the exercise of its powers in governing every department of the Government is not for the public benefit. The Treasury has obtained a position in regard to the rest of the departments of the Government that the House of Commons obtained in the time of the Stuart dynasty. It has the power of the purse, and by exercising the power of the purse it claims a voice in all decisions of administrative authority and policy. I think that much delay and many doubtful resolutions have been the result of the peculiar position which, through many generations, the Treasury has occupied . . . I do not think that the British Constitution as at present worked is a good fighting machine.

Hansard, 4th series, lxxviii, cols. 31-32; 30 January 1900.

(c) HARCOURT'S BUDGET, 1894

Sir William Harcourt's budget of 1894 introduced the new Estate Duty, and with it the principle of graduated taxation.

Sir William Harcourt: . . . Shall a property of £100,000 not contribute on a higher scale than a property of £1,000; a property of £500,000 more than £100,000; and £1,000,000 more than £500,000? This raises in its simplest form the vital question of graduated taxation. To my mind, the principle if applied with fairness and justice is a most equitable and politic principle. Every writer on political economy and finance has laid down the doctrine that taxation should be proportionate to the ability to bear it of those on whom it is imposed . . . Mr Pitt suggested that a man who could afford to keep two carriages should be taxed on each a higher rate than his neighbour who could only afford to keep one. The system of graduation is in force in many of our colonies. In Victoria an estate of £10,000 to £20,000 pays 4 per cent, rising by steps to estates of £100,000, above which 10 per cent is paid. We propose a much more moderate graduation, rising to 8 per cent at £1,000,000, or double the existing maximum . . .

Mr Goschen: . . . As regards the question of graduation, we come there upon what is, no doubt, the newest part of the scheme brought forward by the Chancellor of the Exchequer — new in the sense that such a scheme has never before been proposed to Parliament . . . Schemes for graduation have been placed before Chancellors of the Exchequer by the Inland Revenue Authorities for some years past . . . We must all admit that there is something in the doctrine that increased burdens should be placed upon those who are best able to pay. Graduation introduces this principle and establishes the standard of taxation, not only by the ability of the man to pay, but by the extent of the sacrifice, and it is felt by everyone that there is a greater sacrifice in the case of a man having but £1,000 a year who is called upon to pay £100 than there is in the case of a man with an income of £10,000 a year who would now be required to pay £1,000. There is, no doubt, much to be said in favour of taxing those who are best able to pay, without undue sacrifice, if you can do so fairly and on equitable grounds. I wish it distinctly to be understood that I am not discussing this subject in any final or dogmatic spirit, but I am simply anxious to point out some of the points involved. You get launched here on a new field altogether, where you have no standards to guide you . . . But where are you going to find a standard of what is right to take when you go up to the higher figures? I think that the standards will vary from Parliament to Parliament, and from majority to majority; and the principle of taxation will depend on the wave of public opinion, and not on that equality of taxation which has been insisted upon in our finance . . . I am anxious that this graduation should not become a kind of scaffolding for plunder.

Hansard, 4th series, xxiii, cols. 495, 1130-1132; 16, 23 April 1894.

35 The New Bureaucracy

in Action

Gradual staff wastage as the result of resignations or retirement meant that by the beginning of the twentieth century the vast majority of civil servants had been recruited by open competition. In addition, those who had entered the service by some form of nomination had usually undergone a reasonably rigorous qualifying examination. There was however still no competition for professional posts or for the inspectorates. Certain senior posts were not necessarily filled by promoted civil servants: common grading had still not been accepted for officers above the Second Division. Serious problems remained for the Lower Division clerks who were concerned about their opportunities for promotion. After a question in the Commons in 1894, an extensive correspondence developed on this subject between sixty-five members of the Commons and the Treasury which was determined to retain freedom of action in appointments to the First Division. Despite these problems, the British civil service was moving towards that shape so keenly desired by the Ridley and Playfair Commissions.

The widening range of government activity demanded an able and professional civil service. The establishment of the Board of Education in 1899, which assumed the functions of the Education Department of the Privy Council, of the Science and Art Department and some of those of the Charity Commissioners, was the birth of the first of the new social service departments. The Board of Trade was acquiring vast new powers. Numbers of civil servants increased dramatically: excluding industrial staff, 107,782 established civil servants were employed in March 1902; by 1911 the total had grown to 135,721. The increasing range and quality of government activity also encouraged the gradual extension of the chance for senior civil servants to influence policy. Whereas it was reasonable to see the staff of departments in the first half of the nineteenth century as a body of clerks, the second half of the century saw the emergence of a new breed of permanent secretary. Edwin Chadwick, the innovator and lobbyist, might appear unusual in the 1840s. The parliamentary and departmental demands on a minister had by 1900 increased his dependence on his permanent staff.

200

(a) SIR ROBERT MORANT

At this time, as assistant director of special inquiries and reports in the Education Department, Sir Robert Morant was closely involved in the drafting of the Education Bill, and was shortly to become Permanent Secretary at the Board of Education.

April 1902. Friday's Hill. Sidney had Morant to stay here. Morant is the principal person at the Education Department. He has occupied the most anomalous position the last six months. Taken into office as a nondescript in a humble capacity some years ago, Gorst picked him out for his private secretary. In that way he became acquainted with the politicians — Cabinet Ministers and Conservative private members, who were concerned with Education Bills and education policy. Presently these folk — specially the Cabinet Ministers, found him a useful substitute for Kekewich (permanent head), who was deadly opposed to their policy, and even for Gorst with whom they were hardly on speaking terms, the situation being complicated by the fact that Gorst and Kekewich were complete incompatibles, having no communication with each other! So Morant has been exclusively engaged by the Cabinet Committee to draft this present Bill, attending its meetings and consulting with individual members over clauses, trying to get some sort of Bill through the Cabinet. Both Kekewich and Gorst have been absolutely ignored. Neither the one nor the other saw the Bill before it was printed. Just before its introduction in the House, Morant wrote to Gorst saying he assumed he 'might put his name at the back'. Gorst answered: 'I have sold my name to the Government; put it where they instruct you to put it!' Morant givesstrange glimpses into the working of one department of English government. The Duke of Devonshire, the nominal Education Minister, failing through inertia and stupidity to grasp any complicated detail half-an-hour after he has listened to the clearest exposition of it, preoccupied with Newmarket, and in bed till 12 o'clock; Kekewich trying to outstay this Government and quite superannuated in authority; Gorst cynical and careless, having given up even the semblance of any interest in the office; the Cabinet absorbed in other affairs, and impatient and bored with the whole question of education.

'Impossible to find out after a Cabinet meeting,' Morant tells us, 'what has actually been the decision. Salisbury does not seem to know or care, and the various Ministers, who do care, give me contradictory versions. So I gather that Cabinet meetings have become more than informal — they are chaotic — breaking up into little groups, talking to each other without any one to formulate or register the collective opinion. Chamberlain would run the whole thing if he were not so overworked by his own department.'

Sidney [Webb] and Morant discussed for many hours the best way of so influencing the Cabinet and its advisers that we get a good authority for London. Decided to send out the T.E.B. report widely with personal letters, and to set on foot quiet 'agitations' among the Church folk and other Conservative circles. Among others, Sidney has written a short note to Chamberlain drawing his attention to the policy of 'delegation' in the T.E.B. [report], leaving it to be understood that he would be prepared to delegate management of the elementary schools (properly safeguarded) to borough council committees. Also to Balfour — in fact, I think he has written to every prominent personage, to each according to his views and degree of influence.

Beatrice Webb, *Our Partnership* (Longmans, 1948), pp.239-40.

(b) EYRE CROWE

Crowe was head of the Western Department at the Foreign Office

. . . It remains to consider whether, and to what extent, the principles so elucidated may be said, on the one hand, to govern actual present policy, and, on the other, to conflict with the vital interests of England and of other independent and vigorous States, with the free exercise of their national rights, and the fulfilment of what they, on their part, may regard as their own mission in this world.

It cannot for a moment be questioned that the mere existence and healthy activity of a powerful Germany is an undoubted blessing to the world. Germany represents in a pre-eminent degree those highest qualities and virtues of good citzenship, in the largest sense of the word, which constitute the glory and triumph of modern civilization. The world would be unmeasurably the poorer if everything that is specifically associated with German character, German ideas, and German methods were to cease having power and influence. For England particularly, intellectual and moral kinship creates a sympathy and appreciation of what is best in the German mind, which has made her naturally predisposed to welcome, in the interest of the general progress of mankind, everything tending to strengthen that power and influence — on one condition: there must be respect for the individualities of other nations, equally valuable coadjutors, in their way, in the work of human progress, equally entitled to full elbow-room in which to contribute, in freedom, to the evolution of a higher civilization. England has, by a sound instinct, always stood for the unhampered play and interaction of national forces as most in accord with Nature's own process of development. No other State has ever gone so far and so steadily as the British Empire in the direction of giving free scope to the play of national forces in the internal organization of the divers peoples gathered under the King's sceptre. It is perhaps England's good fortune, as much as her merit, that taking this view of the manner in which the solution of the higher problems of national life must be sought, she has had but to apply the same principle to the field of external policy in order to arrive at the theory and practice governing her action as one of the international community of States.

So long, then, as Germany competes for an intellectual and moral leadership of the world in reliance on her own national advantages and energies England can but admire, applaud, and join in the race. If, on the other hand, Germany believes that greater relative preponderance of material power, wider extent of territory, inviolable frontiers, and supremacy at sea are the necessary and preliminary possessions, without which any aspirations to such leadership must end in failure, then England must expect that Germany will surely seek to diminish the power of any rivals, to enhance her own by extending her dominion, to hinder the co-operation of other States, and ultimately to break up and supplant the British Empire.

Now, it is quite possible that Germany does not, nor ever

will, consciously cherish any schemes of so subversive a nature. Her statesmen have openly repudiated them with indignation. Their denial may be perfectly honest, and their indignation justified. If so, they will be most unlikely to come into any kind of armed conflict with England, because, as she knows of no causes of present dispute between the two countries, so she would have difficulty in imagining where, on the hypothesis stated, any such should arise in the future. England seeks no quarrels, and will never give Germany cause for legitimate offence.

But this is not a matter in which England can safely run any risks. The assurances of German statesmen may after all be no more genuine than they were found to be on the subject of the Anglo-French *entente* and German interests in Morocco, or they may be honestly given but incapable of fulfilment. It would not be unjust to say that ambitious designs against one's neighbours are not as a rule openly proclaimed, and that therefore the absence of such proclamation, and even the profession of unlimited and universal political benevolence are not in themselves conclusive evidence for or against the existence of unpublished intentions. The aspect of German policy in the past, to which attention has already been called, would warrant a belief that a further development on the same general lines would not constitute a break with former traditions, and must be considered as at least possible. In the presence of such a possibility it may well be asked whether it would be right, or even prudent, for England to incur any sacrifices or see other, friendly, nations sacrificed merely in order to assist Germany in building up step by step the fabric of a universal preponderance, in the blind confidence that in the exercise of such preponderance Germany will confer unmixed benefits on the world at large, and promote the welfare and happiness of all other peoples without doing injury to anyone. There are, as a matter of fact, weighty reasons which make it particularly difficult for England to entertain that confidence.

British Documents on the Origins of the War, 1898-1914, edited by G.P. Gooch and H. Temperley, (London, 1928) iii, Appendix A, pp. 406-7.

(c) SIR EDWARD HAMILTON

Sir Edward Hamilton, Permanent Secretary at the Treasury, was previously Gladstone's secretary before becoming a civil servant. His Cabinet memorandum, 'Some Remarks on Public Finance', July 1895, concludes:

. . . that these remarks are not made in any pessimistic, much less alarmist, sense; particularly at this moment when the prospects of an improving revenue are decidedly good. They are intended to be precautionary and to point out that, unless the brake is applied to the spending propensities of the State, which in the last fifteen years have resulted in a growth of public expenditure amounting to no less than £22,000,000, the Government may ere long find themselves confronted with a choice of evils involving serious changes in our fiscal system, and consequently formidable Parliamentary difficulties.

I have finished by Mem. on Budget prospects. There must be increased taxation and the conclusions which I lead up to are (1) that if the Chanc. of the Exchequer wishes to be heroic, he should increase the income tax by a penny, remodel or graduate the House Duty and impose 2/- a quarter or 6d a cwt on Corn; and (2) that if he does not wish to be heroic he should content himself with remodelling and graduating the Income tax and with imposing 1/- a quarter or 3d a cwt on corn. I am convinced that the re-establishment of an old duty which was allowed to continue during the hey-day of free trade down to 1869 will give rise to much less difficulty than the imposition of some new and more or less fancy tax.

Quoted in Roseveare, *The Treasury*, (Allen Lane, 1969), pp. 220-1.

Part Three
WIDER PERSPECTIVES

The problems faced by the British state in the nineteenth century were by no means unique. The transformation of British government from a simple clerkly structure to a complex bureaucratic machine with growing discretionary power was matched by developments elsewhere, in France, Germany, Belgium and the United States of America. England in the sixteenth century and Brandenburg in the seventeenth had experienced the evolution of new administrative forms as a result of the stimulus of social and political change, but although these new forms increased government efficiency they extended the range of government activity very little. It was in the nineteenth century that all advanced societies came to feel the same pressures of industrialization, rapidly rising population and increased urbanization, and had to face the same social problems which provoked some sort of administrative response. As governments found themselves, voluntarily or involuntarily, involved in an ever-widening range of activity, and as individuals encountered government interference more often in their everyday lives, similar questions were raised. How should' the bureaucracy be recruited? Should it be locally or centrally controlled? What should be its relationship with the politicians? Each state resolved the problems presented by the growth of collectivism in its own way within its own traditions. Each profited from the experience of others. It is significant that by the end of the nineteenth century the academic discipline of political science was beginning to emerge from the law and history faculties of the major European and American universities. Max Weber and Samuel Eisenstadt were interested in explaining the causes and consequences of bureaucratization. By the first decades of the twentieth century the shape of the bureaucratic state in the advanced industrial societies was acquiring a familiar outline.

The deployment and seeking of posts in the civil administration by groups in society who were eager to preserve or acquire political and social power appeared in differing guises in Britain, Prussia and the United States. In the early nineteenth century Prussian experience of administrative expertise stood out as unique in Europe and beyond. Able men had, over a long period, been recruited into the Prussian bureaucracy, which had, with the army, come to constitute a powerful élite within the Prussian state. *The Allgemeines Landrecht* of 1794 established a corporate status for the bureaucracy, the *Beamtenstand*, which was separate from those of the aristocratic and bourgeois estates. Noble officials preferred to consider themselves members of the *Beamtenstand* rather than members of the older aristocracy of birth. Noble and non-noble officials formed a coherent élite group which was to a large extent self-perpetuating. Later in the century, the bureaucracy gradually identified itself first with the landowning class and later also with other prosperous groups in society. In the same way that Gladstone had welcomed the Northcote-Trevelyan reforms for their 'tendency to strengthen and multiply the ties between the higher classes and the possession of administrative power' (24a), Prussian landed families seized the opportunities to reinforce their position in society offered by the local and central civil service of Prussia and later in the *Reich*. The empoverishment of many noble estates in the early decades of the century forced their owners to seek employment elsewhere for their sons. If that employment could not be found in the army, it was sought in the civil service. John Gillis has estimated that the number of noble families dependent on each estate had grown from 2:1 in 1800 to 6:1 in the 1880s.[1] This increasing competition for places was also intensified for the *Beamtenfamilien*, the families who had traditionally provided members of the civil service, by the growing tendency for commercial and industrial entrepreneurs to send their sons to universities in order that they might qualify for the civil service. Improvements in the management of noble estates in the 1870s strengthened the position of the younger sons of noble families when they applied for posts where wealth and education were required. In the face of such a heavy demand for posts, conservative reformers could apply stringent social and political criteria when recruiting and promoting candidates. At the same time the universities were becoming less accessible to the poorer sections of society in Prussia. The proportion of entrants with modest means into the civil service declined noticeably during the century.[2] Thus, in a limited sense, the Prussian and later German experience appears to have been the reverse of British development. In the early nineteenth century the system of patronage in Britain had provided civil service posts for young men connected by ties of family and friendship to men in positions of power and influence in much the same way that parliamentary seats were acquired. Suitability for those posts and, indeed, any sort of competence were of only marginal importance. By a slow process, posts in the British civil service became open to anyone who could meet the standards of a competing literary examination. The use of such an examination to test entrants to the civil service derived much from the Prussian experience as adapted to the British academic pattern. In practice, of course, civil service posts were not really 'open' since the examination demanded a standard of education only possible for the more well-to-do groups in British society in the nineteenth century. Nevertheless, with the division of the service into grades, it was theoretically possible, and did occasionally happen, that a man could rise from one grade to another. The structure of the British bureaucracy in 1900 looked rather like that of Prussia at the end of the eighteenth century. The close relationship of interest between the holders of office and the great landowning and industrial families in Germany at the end of the nineteenth century looked a little like that so violently attacked in England in the 1820s and 30s. The confusion of parliamentary and official experience in many German civil servants' careers underlines this parallel. A pre-eminent example of this interchange was the career of Bethmann-Hollweg, who became Chancellor from a civil service background and had sat in the 1890 Reichstag as a Free Conservative deputy.[3]

The attack on the patronage system in Britain in the early nineteenth century and the campaign for recruitment into the civil service by academic tests of ability was matched by the assault on the 'spoils system' in the United States which developed fifty years later and reached its height in the 1870s and 1880s. The American arguments of the later nineteenth century look very much like those of British economical reformers a hundred years before. Oddly enough, during the Napoleonic period, English Radicals held up the American administrative system as a model of efficiency and economy. L.D. White's researches on the period have led him to conclude that 'the moral standards of the Federalist public service were extraordinarily high — higher by far than those prevailing in the British public service or the French and approaching the austerity of the administrative system perfected by Frederick the Great in Prussia'.[4] *The Black Book* in 1820 pointed to the contrast; 'The services which cost America £46,000 a year cost Old England £900,000.' Standards of American administration dropped steadily in the decades after 1800 and a fully fledged 'spoils system' emerged after 1829 with the acceptance of the practice of 'rotation of office'. In the 1840s a succession of purges and counterpurges of officials as party alternated with party formally established a 'spoils system' as part of the American system of government at much the same time as pressures were building up in Britain for administrative reform. It has been argued by Finer that the chief reason that Britain did not experience the same development from a system of patronage to one of spoils lay in the inherent ills and weakness which had been accepted for so long in British government. He sees the financial element in the British patronage system, 'the least defensible feature of the eighteenth century civil service', as 'rendering impossible in the British climate any such doctrine as the rotation of office'. 'Sinecures and reversions', he claims, 'proved a blessing in disguise when they extended, to the minor offices held "at pleasure", the notion that *any* place was a freehold and that on its suppression the holder was entitled to compensation for disturbance.'[5]

The bloated civil list and the unusual irregularities produced by the American civil war focused attention on the problems of administration. Although attempts had been made in the 1840s and 50s to introduce some form of qualifying examination for appointments in the civil service, little was done. Faced with an inefficient and very large civil service, the Secretary of State, William H. Seward, asked John Bigelow, the American Consul-General in Paris, to report on French methods of collecting the customs and was impressed by the competitive examinations used in France in the appointment of customs officers. On 10 April 1864 Charles Sumner introduced a Bill 'to provide for the greater efficiency of the civil service'. It included plans for a board of examiners, competitive examinations, promotion by seniority and for removal only with good cause. It is probable that Sumner's chief motive was to hinder Lincoln's renomination, but there can be no doubt that he was also strongly influenced by contacts with British friends. The Bill received little general support and was dropped. The campaign for civil service reform was then taken up by Thomas A. Jenckes. From his entrance into the House of Representatives in 1863, he studied the problem seriously. He began to correspond with Northcote and Trevelyan and, when he introduced his first Bill in 1865, acknowledged his debt to British experience. This Bill also failed, but in July 1866 the joint select committee on retrenchment was asked to look into questions of civil service recruitment and conditions and also into the expediency of 'withdrawing the public service from being used as an instrument of political and party patronage'. When it was published in May 1868 the elaborate report of this committee provided material for the ensuing debate. It described the existing system in America and included summaries of the administrative systems of China, Prussia, France and England. It also provided a draft Bill intended to adapt some of the advantages of these systems to the American service. Such a reform, a more elaborate form of Sumner's original proposals, was too novel and too sweeping to stand any chance of success. The battle for a more efficient and independent civil service was however joined.

The American civil service reform movement continued into the 1890s. Throughout the argument was confused by the varied aims of the different groups of reformers. The passing of the Pendleton Act in 1883, the first real achievement of the movement, affected only a small proportion of offices. Dorman B. Eaton's work on the British system influenced the debates as did the introduction of competitive examinations for the New York custom house and post office. Examinations were introduced for Washington departments and for custom houses and post offices with more than fifty officials. Hoogenboom contends that much of the impetus for the reform movement came from the disappointment of those without political power, the 'outs'.[6] He demonstrates that Sumner and Jenckes were using civil service reform as a 'weapon . . . which would convert the public service from partisanship to political neutrality'. The way in which the system worked in the 1880s revealed the importance of political manoeuvering. In Britain the main argument for reform had begun with a concern to end patronage, continued with demands for economy and finally concentrated on the need for efficiency. In America the aim was to remove the civil service from the political arena with the achievement of efficiency as a side benefit. In the 1780s in the Commons, criticism of the way in which the King and his ministers deployed patronage was channelled into a campaign for a reduction in the number of offices. In America the attack on the deployment of offices for political purposes focused on the need for competitive examination and promotion by merit. Thus, by the late nineteenth century, the aims of reformers in both Britain and America looked very similar, but the motives that lay behind them were rather different.

American interest in the French administrative system in the 1860s is significant in view of the high degree of centralization in French government. Since the seventeenth century France had become accustomed to regular intervention on the part of the central government at the hands of the *Intendants* who were responsible to the *Conseil d'Etat*. The administrative system created by Napoleon in the period 1799-1804 owed much to that of the *ancien régime*. The new prefects looked much like the *Intendants* but worked without their checks of local and corporate privileges. Napoleon's *Conseil d'Etat* was chiefly composed of paid officials. From these beginnings a centralized civil service and administrative machinery developed which performed most of the functions assumed in Britain by the various organs of local government and in America by the governments of the individual states.

As interest focused on the need for competitive examinations to select members of the new bureaucracies in the industrialized states, decisions had to be made on the desired educational standards to be applied. The styles of the various examinations reflect current assumptions in each society about the necessary training for a budding administrator. Amongst his other administrative reforms, Napoleon created a number of different civil service corps by the establishment of the *grandes écoles*, which were intended to create bodies of highly trained and specialized professional administrators. When he founded the Imperial University he said:[7]

I want to create a corps because such a corps does not die . . . It is necessary that such a corps should have privileges, that it should not be too dependent upon the ministers and upon the Emperor . . . I want a corps that will have an administration and rules so built into the organization of the nation that it will never be possible to dismantle it without due consideration.

Special training for a career in administration remained unique in Europe to France.[8] The only hint of a British experiment in that direction was the setting up of the East India College which later became Haileybury. In Prussia and later in Germany, a legal training was considered essential in addition to university qualifications for a recruit to the civil service. In the early 1880s the length of time candidates were expected to have spent practising in a Law Court was reduced from four to two years.[9] The other two years of probation could be spent in getting practical experience in one of the provincial administrative bodies. A Bill passed in 1902 which became law in 1906 reduced the necessary period in the law courts to one year. Thus throughout the nineteenth century the German civil service was staffed by trained lawyers. About a quarter of the men appointed had taken a doctorate in jurisprudence. By contrast the effect of civil service reform in Britain was to link the qualifying examinations to the courses taught at Oxford and Cambridge. 'Cramming' establishments such as Scoones in Garrick Street still survived to prepare young gentlemen for the diplomatic service, but in general the Order-in-Council of 1870 resulted in higher educational standards in all grades of the civil service.

The role of the bureaucracy in decision making was of course determined by the particular political structure of each state. By the nineteenth century the exercise of administrative initiative was well established in both France and Prussia. By comparison, the dependence by British central government firstly on the unpaid justices of the peace for local administration and later on a varied range of local commissioners appointed to execute particular administrative functions delayed the emergence of a bureaucracy easy in the exercise of administrative discretion. The increasing use of delegated legislation which forced civil servants to take decisions and the increase of discretion granted to such groups as railway and factory inspectors 'in the field' provided opportunities for real influence on the implementation of legislation. Also, as bureaucratic expertise extended, it was to a greater extent taken into account in the drafting of legislation which would set up new organs of government. A machinery of government was being created which, in the twentieth century, would provide ministers with cogent recommendations for new policies or reasoned arguments against proposals coming from outside Parliament. In America similar developments in the Federal government came even later than those in Britain. Whenever societies have experienced administrative change and the increase of government activity, such developments are related to and cannot be divorced from social pressures and political structure. The acceptance by individuals of increasing government interference conveys a great deal about the society from which it springs.

[1]John R. Gillis, 'Aristocracy and bureaucracy in nineteenth-century Prussia', *Past and Present*, 41, (1968) 113. These figures assume that the number of noble families remained constant.

[2]*Ibid*, p.123.

[3]J.C.G. Röhl, 'Higher civil servants in Germany, 1890-1900', *Journal of Contemporary History*, 2 (1967), 119.

[4]L.D. White, *The Federalists: a study in administrative history* (N.Y., Macmillan, 1948), p.514.

[5]S.E. Finer, 'Patronage and the public service: Jeffersonian bureaucracy and the British tradition', *Public Administration*, 30, (1952), 356-7.

[6]A. Hoogenboom, *Outlawing the Spoils: a History of the Civil Service Reform Movement, 1865-83*, (Urbana, Peter Smith, 1968), p. ix.

[7]F. Ridley and J. Blondel, *Public Administration in France*, 2nd ed. (Routledge, 1969), pp.30-1.

[8]For a recent account of the Chinese civil service examinations see I. Miyazaki (translated by C. Schirokauer), *China's Examination Hell: the civil service examinations of Imperial China* (London, Weatherhill, 1976).

[9]Röhl, 'Higher Civil Servants', pp. 102-4.

FURTHER READING

The Controversy

Full bibliographies for material available up to 1970 exist in two review articles in *Victorian Studies*:

CROMWELL, VALERIE, 'Interpretations of Nineteenth-Century Administration', ix (1966), 245-55.

SUTHERLAND, GILLIAN, 'Recent Trends in Administrative History', xiii (1970), 408-11.

General Studies

COHEN, EMMELINE W., *The Growth of the British Civil Service, 1780-1939*, 1941, repr. Cass, 1965.

FRASER, DEREK, *The Evolution of the British Welfare State: a History of Social Policy since the Industrial Revolution*, Macmillan, 1973.

HANHAM, H.J., *The Nineteenth-century Constitution, 1815-1914: Documents and Commentary*, Cambridge U.P., 1969.

PARRIS, HENRY, *Constitutional Bureaucracy: the development of British Central Administration since the Eighteenth Century*, Allen & Unwin, 1969.

ROBERTS, DAVID, *The Victorian Origins of the British Welfare State*, Yale U.P., 1960.

WILLSON F.M.G., 'Ministries and Boards: Some Aspects of Administrative Development since 1832', *Public Administration*, 33 (1955).

Biographies, studies of central and local government

EDSALL, NICHOLAS C., *The Anti-Poor Law Movement, 1834-44*, Manchester U.P., 1971.

FINER, S.E., *The Life and Times of Edwin Chadwick*, Methuen, 1952, repr. 1970.

GILBERT, BENTLEY B., *The Evolution of National Insurance in Great Britain: the Origins of the Welfare State*, Michael Joseph, 1966.

HARRIS, JOSÉ F., *Unemployment and Politics: a Study in English Social Policy, 1886-1914*, Oxford U.P., 1972.

HENNOCK, E.P., *Fit and Proper Persons: Ideal and Reality in Nineteenth-century Urban Government*, Edward Arnold, 1973.

HUGHES, EDWARD, 'The Changes in Parliamentary Procedure, 1880-1882', in Richard Pares and A.J.P. Taylor, eds., *Essays Presented to Sir Lewis Namier*, Macmillan, 1956.

LAMBERT, ROYSTON, *Sir John Simon (1816-1904) and English Social Administration*, MacGibbon & Kee, 1963.

MACLEOD, ROY M., *Treasury Control and Social Administration: a Study of Establishment growth at the Local Government Board, 1871-1905*, G. Bell, 1968.

NELSON, R.R., *The Home Office, 1782-1802*, Duke U.P., 1969.

PELLEW, JILL H., 'The Home Office and the Explosives Act of 1875', *Victorian Studies*, xviii (1974).

PROUTY, ROGER, *The Transformation of the Board of Trade, 1830-1855*, Heinemann, 1957.

ROSEVEARE, HENRY, *The Treasury: the Evolution of a British Institution*, Allen Lane, 1969.

SUTHERLAND, GILLIAN, ed., *Studies in the Growth of Nineteenth-century Government*, Routledge, 1972.

WHEELER, OWEN, *The War Office, Past and Present*, London, 1914.

SMITH, CECIL WOODHAM, *Florence Nightingale, 1820-1910*, Constable, 1950.

WRIGHT, MAURICE, *Treasury Control of the Civil Service, 1854-1874*, Oxford U.P., 1969.

YOUNG, D.M., *The Colonial Office in the Early Nineteenth-century*, Longmans, 1961.

A storehouse of information about, and early twentieth-century attitudes to, the development of individual government departments, their staffing and practices exists in the Whitehall series of studies (Putnam). These were written in the main by serving or just retired senior civil servants and began to appear in the 1920s. They include a wealth of historical material and departmental anecdotes.

FIDDES, SIR GEORGE V., *The Dominions and Colonial Offices*, 1926.

GORDON, HAMPDEN, *The War Office*, 1935.

HEATH, SIR THOMAS L., *The Treasury*, 1927.

LLEWELLYN SMITH, SIR HUBERT, *The Board of Trade*, 1928.

NEWSHOLME, SIR ARTHUR, *The Ministry of Health*, 1925.

SELBY-BIGGE, SIR LEWIS A., *The Board of Education*, 1927.

SETON, SIR MALCOLM C.C., *The India Office*, 1926.

TILLEY, SIR JOHN and GASELEE, SIR STEPHEN, *The Foreign Office*, 1933.

TROUP, SIR EDWARD, *The Home Office*, 1925.

The Royal Institute of Public Administration sponsored a second Whitehall series (published by Allen & Unwin). These were also commissioned from senior civil servants, usually permanent secretaries, but, unlike the original series, tended to focus more on contemporary functions and structure.

BRIDGES, LORD EDWARD, *The Treasury*, 1964.

EMMERSON, SIR HAROLD, *The Ministry of Works*, 1956.

JEFFRIES, SIR CHARLES, *The Colonial Office*, 1956.

NEWSAM, SIR FRANK, *The Home Office*, 1954.

SHARP, DAME EVELYN, *The Ministry of Housing and Local Government*, 1969.

STRANG, LORD, *The Foreign Office*, 1955.

INDEX

Page numbers in **bold** type indicate passages from speeches, writings or books written by or relevant to the subject. References to parliamentary bills or acts are given under the subject or title by which those bills or acts are commonly known. The list of contents provides a quick reference guide to the topics covered.

222

Helps, Sir Arthur, **145-7, 151-3**

Highways, 173

Hitler, Adolf, 58

Hobbes, Thomas, 21

Home Office, 32, 150; duties of home secretary could be divided, idea of Sir Arthur Helps, 146; establishment (1786), 78-81; exclusion from order in council (1870), 149; new legislation to strengthen, 44; salaries of inspectors, 128

Home Rule bill (1893), 175

Hoogenboom, Ari, 212

Household suffrage, unqualified, 29

House of correction, 110

Housing legislation, 52

Huddersfield, 109

Hughes, Edward, 163

Humanitarianism, 30-9 *passim*, 60-5 *passim*

Humboldt, W. von, 68, 70

Hume, Joseph, 24, 50, **101-4**

Hume, L.J., **19-20**

Hunt, Henry, 26

Huskisson, William, 118

Ilbert, Sir Courtenay Peregrine, 186

Income tax, 196

India, 92; office, 153; civil service, 130, 132; *see also* East India

Individualism, 16, 18, 28, 43, 48, 51, 68-9; individualists, 69

'Influence of the crown', 73, 81; waning of, **88-91**

Inland revenue, 199; office, 137 *see also* customs

Intellectual and mechanical labour, distinction between, 138, 140, 149-51, 156; resistance to, 142, 144-5

Intellectual power, need for at head of government departments, 147

Intendants in France, 213

Ireland: bill for promoting university education in (1879), 162; disfranchisement of Irish revenue officers after union with, 90; electoral franchise in, 171-2; home rule bill (1893), 175; land legislation, 171-2; obstruction of parliamentary business, **163-72**; Sir Arthur Helps, commissioner for relief in, 145

Jenckes, Thomas A., interest in American civil service reform, 212

Jenkins, E., M.P., 163

Jenkinson, Robert Banks, *see* Liverpool, second Earl of

Jenkyns, Sir Henry, 186

Johnson, Dr. Samuel, 26

Justices of the peace, 95, 214; staff of, 96

Kay-Shuttleworth, Sir James Phillips, 54, 56; moved from poor law commission service (1839), 56-7

Keeper of the great seal in Scotland, 98

Kekewich, Sir George William, secretary to board of education, 201

Keynes, John Maynard, Baron Keynes, 55

Kitson Clark, G.S.R., 62, 64

Knatchbull-Hugessen, Edward H., first Baron Brabourne, 162

225

228